Kemal Akman

Protecting Against The Unknown

A guide to improving network security to protect the Internet against future forms of security hazards

GRIN Verlag

Bibliografische Information der Deutschen Nationalbibliothek:

Die Deutsche Bibliothek verzeichnet diese Publikation in der Deutschen National-
bibliografie; detaillierte bibliografische Daten sind im Internet über http://dnb.d-
nb.de/ abrufbar.

Impressum:

Copyright © 2000 GRIN Verlag GmbH
Druck und Bindung: Books on Demand GmbH, Norderstedt Germany
ISBN: 978-3-640-80114-5

Dieses Buch bei GRIN:

http://www.grin.com/de/e-book/164385/protecting-against-the-unknown

Protecting against the unknown

A guide to improving network security to protect the Internet against future forms of security hazards

Kemal Akman (Mixter) _____

January 2000

Contents

0   About
0.1   Copyright
0.2   Disclaimer
0.3   Acknowledgements

1   Introduction
1.1   Preface
1.2   Document scope and structure
1.3   Problem description
1.3.1   Security threats summary
1.3.2   Problem definition
1.4   Basic concepts

A short-term approach

2   Conceptual security measures
2.1   Taking the systematic approach
2.2   Designing a security model
2.3   Problems in a corporate environment
2.4   Preparing against an incident
2.5   Incident response
2.5.1   Reacting to an ongoing incident
2.5.2   Post mortem: Incident recovery

3   Technical security measures
3.1   Strong resource protection

3.1.1   Defending your system integrity
3.1.1.1   Setting up a secure environment
3.1.1.2   Establishing access controls
3.1.1.3   Application security
3.1.1.4   Auditing - reactive and proactive measures
3.1.2   Defending your data confidentiality
3.1.3   Defending your network availability
3.1.3.1   Guidelines to defensive routing
3.1.3.2   Tracing: capabilities and problems
3.2   Problem specific protection
3.2.1   Protecting against viruses
3.2.2   Using Intrusion detection systems
3.2.3   Backdoors and trojan horses
3.3   Conclusions about present security technology

A long-term approach

4   Proposed future security architecture improvements
4.1   Improving incident response capabilities
4.1.1   A new approach to incident consulting
4.1.2   Incident response and law enforcement
4.1.3   Establishing an incident response infrastructure
4.2   Operating systems
4.2.1   Privilege separation and kernel-based security
4.2.2   Kernel-based authentication
4.2.3   Privilege and permission separation
4.2.3.1   Sand boxes versus protective cages
4.2.3.2   Differentiated access permissions
4.2.4   Auditing requirements
4.3   Auditing software
4.3.1   Evolving intrusion detection
4.3.2   Evolving proactive auditing technology
4.4   Networking architecture
4.4.1   Routing security
4.4.1.1   Improving availability
4.4.1.2   Improving access controls and authenticity
4.4.2   Protocol security
4.4.3   Public Key Infrastructure
4.5   Improving software design
4.5.1   Technology standards
4.5.2   Network application security
4.5.3   Software development security design methodology

5   Final words

6   Footnotes: technical background, definitions and explanations

0   About this paper

0.1   Copyright

This document was written by Mixter . Technical
solutions, ideas and concepts in this document have mostly been developed by
the author unless referenced or acknowledged otherwise. This paper by Mixter,
named 'Protecting against the unknown', is a candidate entry for the Packet
Storm Security Competition 'Storm Chaser 2000'.
The author hereby represents his eligibility to participate in the
Competition and to satisfy all requirements specified in the Competition
Rules issued by Packet Storm. The author presents that he independently
created the document and waives his intellectual property rights in the
Competition entry. Furthermore, the author has acknowledged, signed and
agreed to all terms of the Packet Storm Affidavit of Eligibility and
Liability and Publicity Release, which has been attached to the submission.

0.2   Disclaimer

This document and the information contained herein is provided on an 'as is'
basis and the author disclaims all warranties, express or implied, including
but not limited to any warranty that the use of the information herein will
not infringe any rights or any implied warranties of merchantability or
fitness for a particular purpose.
Please note that the author's native language is not English. My apologies
in advance in case you should find any formal mistakes in this document.

0.3   Acknowledgements

This paper was improved by many insights I have been able to gain from
a large number of people engaged in the security community. Although the
paper was completely written by myself, knowledge and experience I gained
from these sources were needed to make it possible for me to compose this
document. Some of these sources that I would like to specifically acknowledge
are: Bugtraq Security Mailing List / SecurityFocus, BufferOverflow /
Hackernews, many of the detailed articles from authors of Phrack Magazine,
OpenSEC contributors, site maintainers of security archives and security
related sites, authors of open source security software (no advertisement
here, you know who you are) as well as the authors of publications and texts
referenced in the footnotes section.

1   Introduction

1.1   Preface

Since the Internet has begun evolving from an academic and military resource to a public world-wide computer network utilized by numerous commercial and non-commercial organizations and individuals, and on which modern society is becoming increasingly more dependent, there have been many security [1] issues, some of them exposing weaknesses in the security model of the Internet itself. While the importance of computing will advance in our society, one of the first and biggest problems concerning the evolution of computing is the improvement of applied Internet security technology. With increasing speed and complexity of technology and software development, the number of security issues as well as their severity and impact on the Internet community is tending to grow drastically, and so are the security incidents caused by the growing number of intruders that are actively exploiting weaknesses in current security models and by intrusion software [2] becoming more sophisticated. While defense against specific intrusion software is futile, because private attacking software and techniques can be developed that either can hardly be identified or possess no methodological weaknesses which could be used to stop them, the security problem has to be conquered using coherent, logically applied, systematic security improvement and protection efforts.
This paper attempts to define the problem and answer the question:
  What pure or applied technical measures can be taken to
  protect the Internet against future forms of attack?
In order to develop a defense strategy against future threats, one has to take into account that the proposed solution needs to include effective countermeasures against an unknown threat potential. An approach to this solution needs to be formed upon a differentiated set of measures against current weaknesses and threats, and against upcoming security issues, extrapolated by analyzing existent weaknesses and core problems in the security infrastructure of the Internet. It has to be regarded that current threats like distributed attack tools [3] do not represent security vulnerabilities themselves, but multiply and visualize the potential of existent problems present in the current security architecture model.

1.2   Document scope and structure

The security improvement measures described in this document are designed to provide guidance to everyone who needs to improve the security of his network or machine that is publicly accessible over the Internet, including ISP and corporate technicians, executive managers, government and military executives, network administrators, security consultants and all other individuals requiring or wanting to improve their computer security.
Covered topics include problem and threat definition, potential security issues and active countermeasures, concrete technical requirements and

methods, as well as conceptual and procedural security measures.
To provide a coherent security solution to upcoming and partially yet
unidentified security problems means to design a new security architecture,
instead of trying to solve issues by designing reactive solutions to known
problems. Therefore, this document includes both technical and conceptual
aspects that need to be regarded for the design of a coherent security
architecture.
Since the upcoming threats are serious and imminent, a fast and concrete
solution, which should be practical for everyone is needed. Therefore, the
first part of this paper deals with short-term measures that can immediately
be taken, using the current infrastructure and technological standards.
But it must also be regarded that information technology in general is
still in its infancy, and that a better approach to upcoming, yet
unidentifiable problems and threats has to be realized with long-term
measures aimed at programmers, vendors, corporations, and further instances
responsible for the design of a future information security architecture.
Therefore, the second part of this paper is about such long-term measures
that should be taken to implement future security features and models.
To enhance comprehensiveness of the technical issues, technical definitions
and background explanations have been added in form of footnotes at the end
of the paper. The reader is advised to consult these to help understanding
the definitions and technical subjects mentioned in this paper.

1.3   Problem description

1.3.1   Security threats summary

Before focusing on the problem definition, I would like to summarize the
current actual threats to security and the causes of active security breaches,
possibly correcting or at least questioning some popular viewpoints.
Analyzing opinions shared by authorities and the media, one comes to the
conclusion that malicious software (viruses/worms, trojans, intrusion
software) and intruders which actively spread or use this software are the
cause of all security incidents and therefore represent the major threat to
the Internet.
This is in my opinion a simplistic view of the problem. Imagine the Internet
would consist of 90% vanilla WinNT 4.0 machines (a scary thought..), but no
public exploits existed against them, and no known security weaknesses or
incidents were reported to any authorities. According to the above viewpoint,
there would be no 'threats', even though a single person with appropriate
knowledge would be able to compromise or shut down the majority of the worlds
computers by exploiting just one of the given unidentified weaknesses.
I hope you understood my point that the threat to security should not be
seen in the currently existing malicious software and individuals that take
advantage of mostly known weaknesses to wreak havoc. The threat should be
considered as the damage and incident potential caused by resources [4]
lacking overall security architecture and applied protection. This potential
is also multiplied by the value and possibilities a resource provides to a
potential intruder, once its security is compromised. A compromised web
server for example provides access to all web documents and potentially to
gaining higher privileges on the system. A compromised mail or ftp server
usually provides root access (read: in most cases nearly complete access to
all of the systems capabilities, hardware, network interfaces, hard disk

content, etc.). Observing future trends in the development of the Internet, we could extend our examples to a compromised gigabit ethernet / wdm routing device, giving the advantage of taking up a small countries bandwidth, or a compromised digital wiretapping device used by law enforcement, giving access to privately transmitted information from millions of persons.

To conclude, the value and power of resources are a multiplying factor to the potential of an existing threat, which means that different kinds of resources need different protection, and that delegating resources to a task or service should be done with utmost prudence and care.

However, the origin of security threats can only be seen in the lack of security given for any resource. Such threats include the potential lack of security, in form of uneducated administration personnel, insufficient scrutiny while applying security guidelines and vulnerability to known methods of security compromises [5].

Not existing malicious software, or individuals with malicious intent represent the threats against information systems, but the vulnerability and threat potential that exists in the resources that are to be protected. This shows that responsibility for eliminating security threats lies in the hands of those who are responsible for designing and implementing security.

1.3.2   Problem definition

Taking a look at the current state of security on the Internet, and at the kind of incidents that we have experienced so far, it shows that all serious intrusions, those which involve remote compromise of confidential information, system access and privileges, have all been made possible due to insecure design and implementation of applications or operating system functions and the protocols they use. These problems are present in the input handling, access control, configuration and sometimes the amount of privileges a program requires in order to fulfill its task. While these weaknesses may seem relatively predictable, the cause of intrusions that are and will be frequently occurring has to be seen in a bigger scope.

Consider that actually a high percentage of available servers are secure, and some of them, especially open-source products have been well-audited for several years. There are at least two main reasons that the relatively few programs whose current versions are vulnerable at the same can still be used by intruders to gain access to a huge number of systems:

- Weak configuration and inexperienced users. Today's systems and software that look easy to install and configure are often actually the hardest to establish a secure configuration on, and insufficiently error tolerant (while intolerance to errors means in this context silently creating a major security hole while operating just fine), and either lacks documentation or comes with documentation so complex that the average user does not read it or take the sufficient time to get familiar with the software's functions. This problematic trend causes users and administrators to lack basic experience and understanding of their system programs, including the services running by default on many operating system distributions. Since those systems and their services can be run prior to acquiring information about them, people fail to recognize whether they need particular services or not. Since people can run all these services without spending time with the configuration and documentation, they fail to recognize even simple and well known known vulnerabilities and do not inform themselves about updates or patches.

- Mono-cultural network structures. Another phenomenon that multiplies the chances for intruders and the risks is the fact that a few number of operating system distributions out that come with a static set of applications are widely spread and used, and as a side effect also spread the same known and the yet undiscovered vulnerabilities to a large audience; as a result, one known vulnerability in the today's relatively homogeneous computing environment can become a threat to a large number of similar systems with similar configurations.

Beyond the issues regarding weak operating systems and applications, a further factor that contributes to the problem is the approach of the currently accepted solutions for conceptual software development and security improvement. Today's security measures, applications and protocols are often being standardized with only merchantability, performance and such aspects in mind, and therefore, no coherent systematic design approach is made that includes necessary minimum security standards. With current approaches to technology standardization, other issues like security education of end-users, and extendibility are also being disregarded, which makes it more difficult for software developers to maintain programs complying to those standards, and consequently more difficult to design secure software.

Additionally, ineffective and incoherent concepts to achieving protection against attacks can imply a false sense of security and also represent new opportunities to attackers that are able to find weaknesses in those concepts. For example, security through obscurity empowers those who are able to crack and reverse engineer software. Relying on law enforcement gives an opportunity to those who can withdraw from law enforcement. Extensive intrusion pattern logging, and origin tracing can be a disadvantage to inexperienced intruders but an advantage to the intruders that use private exploits and have enough compromised machines at their disposal to obscure their origin.

Only implementation of all basic and systematic protection measures can effectively withstand all current and upcoming threats.

1.4   Basic concepts

Before coming to applied security measures, I want to briefly describe some of the basic concepts that can be used to assess a solution and which can be applied to design a systematic approach.

To start off, it is advisable to find the lowest layer of information processing to which security measures can be applied to. Excluding physical security and hardware design, the lowest layer of security has to be established at the operating system level; for the existence of access control [6] to any resource and system capability, it is required that this control can be securely enforced by the operating system on which it is implemented. The next layer is the secure transmission and storage of data in general - locally and remotely. Note that access control has to be in place for this layer to effectively work [7]. An effective additional measure to harden this security layer can be cryptography, because of its universal applicability. Further security layers are problem specific, in this case network specific. The third layer of network security is the stability and security of any points of access [8] to a network, single machine or higher privileges.

Only by ensuring presence of such a consecutive row of security layers to protect against a problem, it is possible to construct a scalable solution, whose protection can then be improved at its weakest layer, if necessary. Another paradigm for establishing a long-term security solution is easy implementation feasibility, realized by avoiding unnecessary complexity and minimizing the efforts needed to individually adapt the solution. To achieve this, steps have to be taken to design standards which are more comprehensible and easier to implement, especially regarding recommended use of programming style and functions, and the design of security API, system security capabilities, protocols features and other security interfaces.

2 Conceptual security measures

2.1 Taking the systematic approach

People are well advised to put their efforts into achieving one goal: optimizing network security to mitigate the vulnerability potential over a maximum period of time. The second rule to follow is to use common sense and apply logical concepts. An untrusted system, i.e. a system that could already potentially have been compromised cannot totally be 'secured'. Refrain from connecting a vanilla (out-of-the-box, as some people say) system to any network, before applying basic security guidelines. An intruder could theoretically be getting into it while you are in the process of securing it, rendering all your efforts worthless. And if we are talking about a high profile system or a popular attack target, this applies even more. Either a system has been secured from the beginning or it can never be considered to be fully trusted. Things that should be established from the beginning on also include some form of backup/recovery system, at least for unique data, and some kind of checksums or change logs, preferably cryptographic, which will later be valuable resources to compare the systems current state with its original state reliably.

In order to eliminate vulnerabilities efficiently, try compiling a vulnerability checklist, ordered by priority. Security threats considered as critical to a systems survival have to be eliminated at all costs. Do not take easily preventable risks either (e.g. by not updating software versions or configuration to latest standards). A good administrator should try to imagine worst case situations. If someone could be interested in gaining as much access to your network as possible, don't be scared to imagine what could happen if someone would successfully run a sniffer. Measures like using switched ethernet are easy to apply and should be mandatory (although be warned that this might only raises the difficulty level; using ARP cache poisoning, sniffing is still feasible), and critical devices such as switches, routers, gateways and other packet forwarding devices, as well as log hosts and other hosts that serve the function to preserve your network / data integrity should not be accessed remotely at all; ideally they have no open ports at all and must be accessed via console. A few weeks earlier I would've suggested running ssh as only service, but since a working exploit against a current version of ssh is out... well, by assuming the worst case in all situations applicable to your network, you cannot be wrong.

2.2 Designing a security model

Just like a single host that has to be protected prior to using it in a

network environment, internal structural design of your network(s) has
to be completed before exposing them to the Internet.

Taking a look at the latest threats, and upcoming possibilities of intruders,
I would strongly advise a decentralized task security model. This means to
avoid single, big resources that share many points of access. On one hand,
hosts that run a concentrated amount of services can be easier compromised
because an intruder can select from a variety of services which to exploit,
and on the other hand, by having a single, big machine compromised or
penetrated with Denial Of Service [9] attacks over a long time, you would
lose a lot of services at a time, which possibly many users or critical
network processes depend on.

Consider using a higher bandwidth on your local network than you have overall
bandwidth to your uplink(s), so you still would have the possibility of
internal process and user communication when your network gets hit by DoS
from the outside.

Try to retain the systematic aspect of design. Reliable audit trails are good,
preventive measures against intrusions are much better. Do not rely on an
extra mechanism if you know that your networks security would be lost without
it. Once you have established basic security, extra packet filtering and
intrusion detection rules can act as additional security layers if deemed
necessary. Another subject worth mentioning is a mistake which I have
observed is being frequently made. Yes, a DMZ is supposed to be exposed to the
Internet more than the other sensitive parts of your network are. But that
does not mean there is any reason in exposing hosts on the DMZ, preferably
mail servers, bastion hosts, and gateways running a bulky mass of services,
to preventable risks! This is something just too many people do, without
considering that the DMZ hosts are very vital parts of your overall network
security. I would bet that more than a half of all incidents have happened on
those hosts, which have been poorly secured or not secured at all, while their
protection is as important as protection of any other network components.

2.3   Problems in a corporate environment

A popular, generally accepted security solution for corporations is to
establish a security policy, and then assign a team that is specially
responsible for protecting the corporate resources and enforcing that
policy. The problem is that a few people in control of security measures
cannot guarantee this protection, while the rest of the employees possibly
lack sufficient understanding of their software to care enough about security.
The same way in which it is possible to demonstrate lack of security, but
not its guaranteed existence, a security policy can be enforced with all
technical measures, but cannot fully guarantee that employees lacking
awareness find a way to circumvent it (or that the policy is not sufficient
and people never find out about it). A better approach to corporate security
is to define a minimum of security and of technical education for everyone,
and educate everyone in an adaptive manner, suiting the individually present
state of knowledge. Instead of possessing either expensive or insufficient
security, corporate security needs to be designed to be comprehensible for
everyone, and education that goes beyond basic mandatory guidelines should be
acquired individually by self-education; that way, corporate security can be
achieved by everyone without dedicating it huge amounts of money or time.
Taking this approach, however, makes it necessary to observe how well it is
individually adapted, rewarding knowledgeable employees with respect, and
helping those who face problems gaining the sufficient knowledge, possibly by

assigning them to teams with more knowledgeable individuals.

2.4   Preparing against an incident

To be prepared against incidents like intrusions, intrusion attempts, and DoS
coming from outside your local network, it is important to be able to
correctly interpret the meaning of probes [10] and other unusual traffic to
your network, and of course to have sufficient audit trails present that can
be evaluated. Some essential precautions that should be taken are to enable
network egress and ingress filtering [11], and setting up secure, impenetrable
logging facilities, in form of a more or less isolated loghost [12].
By being able to recognize the kind of threat, you prevent unnecessary panic
when you are facing futile intrusion attempts, and on the other side can
take appropriate measures quickly, when your systems are really at risk.
Preparation should generally start at network design, in form of separating
important tasks of the network by delegating them to different machines with
the aim to minimize the damage that can be caused by an incident.
While in my humble opinion there are not many similarities between computer
crime and conventional crime, one thing they have in common is that they can
hardly be stopped by harder prosecution and better tracking. If an intruder
wants to gain access to your network, and there is any possibility, he will.
Like conventional crime, the better approach to mitigating the possibility
that incidents occur is to make an intrusion into your network appear less
inviting by hiding as much information about your network as possible.
Approaches to this include using meaningless hostnames for different
internal hosts that serve different purposes, denying external DNS zone
transfer, configuring your servers to show bogus version information, or even
slightly modifying your kernel to defeat remote OS identification [13]. While
this tactic does not represent a factual security improvement, you will stop
presenting a possible intruder information about where to find your internal
DNS server, SQL databases, and other weak points on a golden plate. Note
that the best method in making your host an uninviting target is of course
to apply all possible security measures at your disposal. A final important
preparation is to have some way of recovery, in form of incremental backups,
site mirroring, or anything else you deem appropriate, and to possess
necessary information to reestablish integrity of your critical data, in
form of cryptographic checksums and/or system images of a trusted state of
your systems, which have to be stored in a way that it is not possible for
an intruder to remotely manipulate them.

2.5   Incident response

2.5.1   Reacting to an incident

If your router experiences large amounts of spoofed traffic, it is recommended
to ask your uplink or backbone provider for assistance. In all other cases
that represent a real threat to your network, you are well advised to directly
contact the responsible technical or administrative authority of the attackers
origin(s). While the current international chain of network information
centers is undergoing structural changes, there are still reliable ways
to find the proper authority to contact. A WHOIS hostname query to

whois.internic.net will, in most cases, reveal the proper NIC to contact. [14]
If this is not the case, you should try contacting whois.ripe.net for
European IP addresses, whois.apnic.net for Asia, and whois.arin.net, which
will always deliver you information about the owners of assigned IP blocks.
If the contact persons you found do not reply to email and phone in a short
period of time, look up their uplink provider by querying whois.arin.net,
doing traceroutes, or by gathering information about the hosts that provide
top-level DNS services to them, generally shown in the WHOIS query. Another
possibility is to make use of the Network Abuse Clearinghouse, by sending
email to @abuse.net, which will efficiently try to
contact the responsible administration, especially if you are experiencing
unauthorized use of your mail servers.
If you are experiencing ongoing intrusions which are massively putting
machines on your network at risk (e.g. you are experiencing repeated buffer
overflow attempts that indicate the attacker only needs to find the correct
offset, you are not certain if low-privilege access has already been gained,
your webserver is being intensively probed and you are not convinced that it
is totally secure, or a front-door brute force password cracking attack is
going on), emergency actions should be filtering the attackers subnet at the
border routers, and if the attacker is persistent, temporarily null-routing
or even shutting down attack victims and other weak hosts on the network.

2.5.2   Post mortem: Incident recovery

Once your security has been partially or completely compromised, you have
two proposed solutions to recovery, with the goal of restoring the system
back to a trusted state. The first, and most reliable solution is to do a full
backup from the last trusted system state [15], or, if backup data is not
present, to completely delete and reinstall the system, only retaining
databases, documents and other non-executable data from the compromised
system. The second approach means to examine your system to find the
path an intruder has taken in compromising, backdooring and using your system.
You should have some kind of checksum data present in this case, to find
changed binaries. Checksums and checking utilities have to be kept on a
device that cannot be manipulated, such as a removable disk. If you assume
the worst case, your system kernel or libraries could be changed in order
to hide checksum errors. You can, however, keep checksums on each machine,
if you encrypt or digitally sign them with a key that is not stored in any
form on the machine, e.g. with PGP or any other strong encryption tool. [16]
Performing initial integrity verification of the checksums from a trusted,
non-compromised system (or by booting from removable media), is mandatory.
After that you are able to isolate and examine changed files. Popular
backdoors that you should scan for in the first place to reveal starting
points of a compromise include system configuration such as inetd.conf,
SysV init scripts, access control lists, password files, shell profile files,
rhosts files, crontabs, server and other critical system binaries, as well
as hidden filenames (find / -type f -name "*[ ]*" -o -name "*.*.*") and
files in unusual places (find /dev -type f). Further methods that can help
you analyze what steps and intruder has taken are all instances of logging
facilities, which should be closely analyzed from the first possible event
of intrusion. After restoring a system back to a trusted state, the
vulnerability that has been used to gain access has to be identified and fixed
at all costs, together with all obviously existing weak points in the security
design that have lead to the vulnerability not being discovered and patched
before. Keep in mind that a vulnerability can be everything from an

exploitable server to insecure access permissions or weak passwords.

3   Technical security measures

3.1   Strong resource protection

In retrospect, attacks against information systems, be it embedded technology,
telephone networks or computer networks have been commenced for a long time on
a tame, mostly experimental and educational basis. Of course, malicious intent
has always been present, but because of computing still being in a relatively
early phase, the challenge to break security has not yet been high enough to
make military-level intrusion skills for an intruder necessary to be able to
compromise enough resources to satisfy his or her needs. With the necessity
of protection becoming popular, and countermeasures against intrusions
advancing, we are about to experience equal advancements in intrusion
technology as an adequate answer of the intruders who want to be able to
compromise resources, be it for gaining knowledge, financial profit,
or because of social, military or terrorist ambitions.
To keep up with this trend, the strongest protective measures currently
available should be applied by everyone to defend their resources, because
on the Internet, all resources are theoretically being targeted equally. The
following section will make an attempt to establish a universal guide to
defining and applying existent security measures to your network environment,
by identifying defense methods for separate points of access and bringing
them together as a scalable technical solution. To retain the independent
applicability of this solution, I will evade recommending operating system
specific solutions or products; additionally, a paper describing such a
specific solution would require constant improvement and updates when
specific vulnerabilities would be discovered or functionality of specific
software would be improved.

3.1.1   Defending your system integrity

Possessing system integrity means having functional access control, a trusted
and secure environment and control over any modifications made to the data
belonging to you. Points of access that can be used for attacks against
system integrity include all processes involving evaluation of data -
sessions, informational and executable content - performed by the kernel,
servers, applications and scripts.

3.1.1.1   Setting up a secure environment

In the beginning, the operating system has to be in the most secure condition
that is possible. If your system allows it, recompile your kernel, applying
all patches relevant to security and stability, and disable capabilities that
you will not need. Enabling firewalling, resource limits and using restrictive
network features (regarding spoof- and flood protection as well as routing

and packet forwarding) are especially recommended.
If you have a personal choice of what operating system, distribution and release version to prefer, there are some important recommendations you should consider. Naturally, use of systems that have proven to contain very little vulnerabilities over a long time and are open-source should be preferred [17]. Systems offering a minimum of pre-configured settings and programs, which have to be customized manually often offer a maximum of stability and security to the knowledgeable user (see problem definition, 1.3.2), for example systems belonging to the BSD family, but also other Unix systems or Linux, if installed with a minimum of pre-configuration and pre-installed applications. Another important security criteria when selecting an operating system (or any other software, for that matter) is not to use very recently published software for production, because most present vulnerabilities of a distribution or other software product are still being found after its release. Therefore, it is recommended using older operating system versions with all released vendor patches and updates for production. [18] Before going any further, it is important to consider that protecting a multi-user system is much harder than a single user system. If you are establishing protection on a dedicated mail/web/ftp/etc. server, disabling nearly all accounts, including anonymous mail and ftp access, and setting up restrictive access control (see 3.1.1.2) makes the task easier.
On multi-user systems, your tasks must include proper local resource and access restriction (using quota, securelevels, permission checking scripts, systems security- and limit configuration files), and mitigating the chances for a local security compromise by disabling suid permissions where not explicitly necessary and updating remaining critical suid applications.
To establish a secure environment, one more thing to do is to ensure that no modification to the files that you expect to be trusted, by using simple Perl or other scripts (I like Tcl a lot) that ensure file integrity. This should include checking of size, access and modification time, detecting recently created files in paths reserved for privileged accounts, and cryptographic checksum comparison. This is basically the job of host-based intrusion detection, whose purpose is to detect irregularities that can be signs of security compromises. To really ensure data integrity, cryptographic checksum comparison has to be commenced from a completely trusted environment, such as a write protected removable media from which is booted and which contains all files necessary to validate checksum information. To be able to actually trace back and recover from occurred unattended modifications, there is no other way than having data recovery mechanisms present (be it in form of high-level RAID, full backups, or regular site mirroring).

3.1.1.2 Establishing access controls

Before thinking about any kind of (password-) authentication, basic measures should be established that narrow down the amount and range of clients that can connect to your hosts or specific services. Access to services that are being used only internally, e.g. POP, portmap, or SNMP, should be blocked at your border router - specific configuration depends on how you are using your network, however, for most small web sites there is not much that speaks against only permitting incoming http traffic. Secondly, restrictive local access control should be established. If you can, permit only sessions from explicitly trusted hosts. For services run via inetd/tcpd and portmap, the access permissions are set in hosts.allow (while denying all default traffic in hosts.deny, if using restrictive controls), for other services there are separate access configuration files that need to be modified. The advantage of blocking lies also in the fact, that denied connections can be logged and help indicate possible security violation attempts. If really fail-safe audit trails are desired, nothing beats running tcplogd, udplogd and icmplogd running together with a syslog daemon that forwards all traffic to a loghost. A dominating rule for access control of any kind should be to enforce the predetermined security requirements by the system, not relying on users to uphold system security.

The same rule applies to all kinds of password-based authentication. While buffer overflow and other exploits have been gained popularity to overcome system protection, during times where less vulnerabilities are being exposed, attacks against the weak password authentication scheme should never be underestimated. [19] Therefore it is mandatory for the authentication system to enforce the use of strong passwords by everyone, especially root, and password aging - to prevent compromise due to sniffing or successful attacks against individual users. [20]

3.1.1.3 Application security

The core of the currently present security problems certainly revolves around deficits in the countless and complex server and client applications, which often possess security relevant bugs. While there is no definite solution and no final proof for the security of an application, evolving incident response capabilities and full-disclosure security are helping to discover information about serious issues earlier, a situation of which you should take advantage by frequenting security- and your vendors sites to periodically gain knowledge about latest serious vulnerabilities, install patches, and if your system has been exposed for a long time by containing a serious bug, performing integrity verification and intrusion checking measures. Regarding the technical aspect, understanding a program means being able to detect security issues, and browsing its source code for known security leaks [21] is recommended, if the application is in beta development stage, or a security critical application used on many of your networks machines. World Wide Web related traffic is a specifically fragile topic, because it is often used for gaining access to system whose overall protection is relatively strong. By being able to chose exploits from a huge collection of existing vulnerabilities in HTTP servers, Server Side Includes, and CGI scripts an intruder has many possible starting points for compromising security. It is important to consider every CGI script and similar facilities belonging to the web server as a single server application, because they are executables that are evaluating remote content on the web servers machine. Be very careful while configuring the HTTP servers runtime permissions and minimize the amount of CGI scripts, for example by using Java or similar content to enhance a web sites appearance at the clients end, just like you should minimize the number of other servers that you run off your site.

Upcoming reactive solutions to provide application security are represented by applications that try to harden the operating systems protection against common security vulnerabilities, by restricting processes' access to resources (like special files, memory page segments and kernel capabilities) and issuing alerts when access to such resources is attempted. Examples include StackGuard and Unix kernel patches to protect stack segments and internal registers, and stack shield, a compiler wrapper that produces binaries with self protection against boundary overflow attacks by wrapping the compilation at assembly level. Obviously, these are only temporary solutions against a specific (but widespread) problem category, but show that the problem has to be solved by improving security measures at operating system level. Nevertheless, it is strongly recommend to make use of these solutions for now and make use of intensive auditing to compensate the existent weaknesses.

3.1.1.4 Auditing - reactive and proactive measures

To provide coherent security, the process of auditing has to be applied frequently, to improve not only the security of applications, but of all substantial and abstract parts information systems consist of.
Reactive auditing means a constant verification that preventive and protective measures are sufficient by improving configuration and design of systems, software and network design. An important part of this task is to routinely identify and evaluate occurring events on a system, to be able to discover vulnerabilities as they are exploited or created. Therefore, auditing should start at kernel level, in form of detailed verification and ability to record all of the systems actions, independent from logs generated by applications themselves, because they can never fully be trusted, as shown. Platform specific experimental approaches exist in form of the system events logger ssyslogd, or the kernel-level execution logging lkm exec.c, but current kernel based event logging are not yet standardized, or implemented into operating systems, so that secure kernel-level auditing is problematic. It is generally advisable to make use of auditing and intrusion detection tools that work on a remote, networked basis, to enhance reliability and availability of audit trails in critical events. If you want resource protection at the strongest level possible, a currently possible solution you should consider is auditing using remote real-time auditing agents (IDS, data verification- or event monitoring applications capable of transmitting traffic to a central evaluating machine) and half- or fully automated real-time traffic and signature processing to be able to react to all events threatening system integrity immediately. If such agents are used, and it is technically possible to disable remote management facilities, it should be done, to provide a safe one-way reporting channel without opening a possible point of access. [22] Besides all these sophisticated measures, you should never forget to implement the proactive aspect of auditing, which means to systematically scan your system remotely (and locally if necessary) for exploitable vulnerabilities. Proactive auditing is so advisable because it means to examine your systems from the 'black-hat' viewpoint of an intruder, meaning with the goal in mind to be able to gain unauthorized access to it. You might always have forgotten some updates or configuration changes, leaving a critical hole open, and therefore combined reactive and proactive auditing is necessary to mitigate the possibilities for an intrusion. See also [23].

3.1.2 Defending your data confidentiality

Ensuring confidentiality of your data means to effectively protect sensitive and private information of any kind, stored on and transmitted over systems that are connected to the Internet, from being accessed by any external party. Pre-requirement is to possess an environment with intact integrity of data and functional access control mechanisms, to prevent leaking out of confidential information from a supposedly trusted storage source.
For accomplishing this task, cryptographic measures are essential. Wherever possible on a network, services using plaintext authentication and sessions should be completely disabled and replaced with equal services supporting encryption, like ssh for telnet and r-commands, sftp for ftp, SSL instead of base64 encoded plaintext basic authentication for web servers, and kerberos

authentication instead of plaintext authentication for services like POP, IMAP, and nntp. While plaintext services seem to be a bigger threat to privacy than to effective system security, they aren't. A huge number of intrusions commenced by knowledgeable intruders are performed by gaining access to a huge number of machines all around the world, installing stealthy packet sniffing programs with the purpose to gain as many login / password information as possible, hoping to gain access to high-profile systems which are then invaded and compromised by attacking local system security. Additionally, a compromise of authorization methods can be used to gain access to trusted resources. Basic authorization is realized at protocol level, and therefore protection against attacks that involve spoofing has to be present. While vanilla IP spoofing is itself no confidentiality issue and cannot be prevented, security of TCP sessions should be improved by assuring that all trusted systems use unpredictable TCP sequence numbers, to prevent tcp hijacking. Another vulnerability lies in the ARP (ethernet address resolution protocol). Dynamic ARP cache entries can be manipulated using forged ARP traffic; use of static ARP cache entries, especially on routers and switches is recommended, to prevent malicious packet redirection to arbitrary hosts. Once the security on a system is compromised, session hijacking and sniffing from a client process' memory is quite feasible, for example by using process tracing. While the use of programs like SSH is strongly recommended, another important factor is keeping contact to system administration of other remote trusted systems, making sure that their system security is not the weakest link in your chain of resource protection.

Further methods of providing confidential transmission of data include using IPSEC tunneling and IPv6 protocol capabilities, and similar protocol based solutions, as well as Virtual Private Networking, all of which are generally advantageous to use, but cannot be fully recommended yet to be used by everyone because of today's lacking standardizations, public key infrastructure and wide-range implementation in operating systems and applications.

To assure local data confidentiality, which can, in addition to assuring privacy and anonymity, play an important role to prevent user-level attacks against data and privileges of other user or administrator accounts, I would advise reading [24].

3.1.3   Defending your network availability

Assuring availability on your network means to protect your communicational in form of a guaranteed minimum bandwidth and impenetrable functionality of processes which use remote data transmission. To define requirements for a defense is a delicate task, because for an attacker, the potential of Denial Of Service [9] attacks often depends on gaining access to any host(s), which do not have to be associated with your network at all [25]. In the beginning, possibilities for attacks which an attacker could perform with minimal efforts have to be eliminated. As mentioned in 3.1.1.1, your systems should be prepared against application- and kernel-level (including IP protocol stack) attacks, by having applied specific vulnerability and flood protection patches, for example in form of a robust syn cookie implementation [26]. To prepare against Denial Of Service, distributing tasks over different hosts is an invaluable method of minimizing impact of (wanted or unwanted) traffic irregularities and problems, because the number of unavailable services during such periods are minimal, and an attacker would have to concentrate on many targets. If administrating a larger network, separating network segments via routing, packet filtering capable device can make sense, to generate zones of different availability, which will help you to set different priorities on a network, along with using more than one uplink channel at different spots of your network, raising the chance of being able to have emergency or spare bandwidth to the rest of the world in case of ongoing massive flooding attacks.

The next important thing to do is to secure your routing infrastructure, by preventing intrusions made by spoofed or unauthorized routing protocols coming from an attacker. It is generally advisable to only accept ICMP, TCP and UDP traffic to prevent arp, rip and other fragile protocols to penetrate your internal hosts and routers. This also applies to closing down tcp/udp ports used for routing at your network border, if using for example routed (udp) or routers running border gateway protocol (tcp). If you rely on a firewall/gateway solution for blocking outside access, it is advisable not to allow outgoing ICMP/11 (time exceeded) messages, which can be used to map your protected network, even if most tcp/udp ports are being blocked [27].

3.1.3.1 Guidelines to defensive routing

From a strong security perspective, routing should have the ability to prevent traffic that could be malicious or unwanted from entering or leaving a network and perform this task with a minimum of extra routing features and access rules, which could degrade the routing performance during high bandwidth traffic, possibly caused by attacks, and represent potential weaknesses, as increased complexity always does in a network environment.

Routing and packet forwarding/switching should never be allowed on firewalling and gatewaying machines that process packets themselves, because it could be exploited to bypass gateway and firewall rules, penetrating internal hosts. One of the most important things (which everyone should know about anyway) is to disable outgoing directed broadcast traffic that can give an attacker the opportunity to use your networks broadcast replies to generate icmp and udp broadcasts storms directed against another victim (smurf / fraggle attacks). Using SNMP capabilities of routers can be advantageous to detect and respond to irregularities or possible intrusions, but should be done with care, as securely configuring this facility is absolutely critical [28]. If you are inexperienced with SNMP and don't already have a concrete concept of using it to gather statistical network information, you are well advised to disable it. Further extra routing capabilities (like Cisco's CDP, debug mode, link state routing) should not be activated, especially not on border routers, unless particularly necessary, with the exception of tcp intercept features [29]. If bandwidth and availability is critical for your network, or if your uplink charges you depending on the amount of traffic sent, it is advisable to establish especially restrictive access rules at network borders by blocking most in- and outgoing ICMP datagram types if unnecessary for your internal network tasks (especially unreachables, which can help to multiply effects of DoS attacks and udp probes), and to deny access to privileged ports on which internal services are run or which are not needed to be accessed by external hosts at all [30]. Additionally, you should evaluate your router logs and examine status information on your routers periodically, to detect networking problems, and eventually change to restrictive or emergency access lists you have previously compiled, for the case that network critical events occur.

3.1.3.2 Tracing: capabilities and problems

Origin tracing is a measure essential to network protection and incident response. In the context of packet switching based networks, it means to reliably determine the origin of incoming packets, including packets with forged IP source addresses. Determining the origin of incoming forged packets is necessary to contact the proper administrative authorities for the network(s) or host(s) from which an attack - mostly packet flooding DoS attacks - is coming in order to stop the attacks by either fixing security leaks on systems which the attacker is using or by getting attacking systems taken off the network.

One method of generating audit trails on your routers, that help in improving tracing capabilities, is to establish ACL rules that permit, but log traffic that matches patterns which are commonly found in DoS attack traffic [31]. However, by instructing your routers to generate extensive logs, possibly using extensive ACL rules, you are risking to cripple your routing performance and actually decrease your capacities.

To sites for which it is critical to be able to establish tracing capabilities, be it for network observation or incident response ability, I would recommend to do the following: at your network border, set up routers that do plain IP based routing with a minimum of enabled access rules and features. The border routers should then, additionally to routing traffic, forward all traffic to a separate router, which null-routes all incoming packets and is only used for forensic purposes. This 'forensic' router then has all facilities and features enabled that help evaluating the traffic and creating valuable audit trails. This router can be slowed down, because it is not dedicated to routing, but only to evaluating and auditing traffic. Note that this is of course only a solution recommended for big companies and backbone providers who can afford running such an infrastructure.

Additionally, your routers should make use of NTP (network time protocol), because tracing relies on a time-based correlation of log events, and slight time differences can already complicate log evaluation (for example, if you have to evaluate a huge amount of packets, each with a different forged source IP address, that have been transmitted in a short amount of time). The above measures are meant to help tracing packets using hop-by-hop tracing, which means to trace packet streams by evaluating the routing entries of each router between source and destination host. A packet with a forged IP address is followed back by determining from which port it entered, and then continuing the trace on the router associated with that port, until reaching the origin. This is hard to do because it requires all involved uplinks to coordinate in performing the trace over their backbone, and it has to be performed quickly, because the routing entries are automatically cleared shortly after a finished or failed host-to-host connection.

See Figure 1 [32] for a scenario of tracing back a distributed attack.

Another way of associating incoming packets having forged source IP addresses is to identify them by MAC (media access control layer, usually ethernet) addresses, which are generally not spoofed. Using IP debugging features on a router, one can determine the MAC addresses of incoming packets, and save them for reference and later backtracing or compile access control lists on all border routers that deny and log packets with the concerning MAC addresses, if technically supported.

3.2   Problem specific protection

Despite all efforts to improve overall security by properly protecting and maintaining a site's resources, risks to become a victim of new or unresolved vulnerabilities or general weaknesses present in the network architecture may be mitigated, but not eliminated. Yet undiscovered and non-public vulnerabilities might exist in popular server software, that are not being detected despite of performed source code auditing. A fundamental security flaw could be present in your core operating system or protocol stack, temporarily rendering all security efforts useless. You might become a target of attacks which exploit fundamental weaknesses of the current Internet architecture, including DNS and PKI hierarchic structures [33], protocol weaknesses, and resources of other, insecure systems turned against you [34]. Therefore, it is required to adopt strategies to prevent and recognize ongoing events endangering system security and emergency methods to stop such events.

3.2.1   Protecting against viruses

Since the aim of this paper is to help protecting your network against new kinds of attacks, what is my point of coming up with viruses? Actually, virus related problems and problems caused by system insecurity and intrusions have some points in common, especially regarding their evolution and effective countermeasures against them. A virus is a pattern that self-replicates and tends to be spread to other systems from infected ones, be it by exploiting weaknesses of the system, or weaknesses of the systems communication infrastructure (i.e. using human interaction or popular distribution channels in a network to spread). So, viruses take advantage of the infected systems to penetrate further systems from there, meaning that they actually belong in the category of distributed attack tools (though they are not human-controlled and thus target random victims).
The interesting thing about virus and worm code is that there are few limitations regarding its possible appearance. It can exist in virtually infinite new forms, and use an infinite amount of new methods to propagate and operate, making detection a hard task [35]. The current anti-virus solution is to maintain pattern databases of today's known viruses and scan for their occurrence. However, pattern scanning is obviously a futile method against viruses, since an infinite number of new viruses with new patterns can be created. This is also the reason of virus outbreaks despite widely used and updated Anti-Virus software, as caused by the Melissa worm, CIH, BubbleBoy, etc. After the outbreak of such threats, they can be recognized, but this is an insufficient security strategy which people should not rely on. If I wanted to spread a virus, I wouldn't have to write an entirely new one. Implementing unknown or modified self-encrypting algorithms into a virus and deploying the encrypted version would suffice, as not a single scanner can actually detect or reverse engineer encrypted viruses.
(Fine, they can scan for the self-decryption code once they've seen it and updated databases, but that won't help a scanner discovering it initially). A somewhat better solution is heuristic program analysis, which detects what kind of functions and resources a program is designed to use, determining virus-like character. Again, those scanners don't detect encrypted viruses. As I mentioned in section 1.3.2, solutions like present anti-virus scanners give people a false sense of security. Once they run updated scanners, they often assume to be 100% safe, and happily access untrusted binary executable content. Instead, the solution needs to be based upon restrictive guidelines. Applications (and all content that will be evaluated and executed by interpreters or as machine code) need to be either coming from a trusted source, compiled locally from source code that can openly and freely be reviewed before compiling and running it, code running with a drastically reduced set of permissions and system access, or else they must not be executed at all costs. Since this is especially hard to realize with current

desktop operating systems and software models, new software standards and operating system requirements have to be formulated to effectively cover security deficits in present software technology, as proposed in section 4.2.

3.2.2 Using Intrusion detection systems

Host- and network based intrusion detection can be described as a set of methods for discovering attack signatures in network traffic and system data. The above introduction to viruses and problems that are encountered in the development of countermeasures helps to show the parallels that exist with the IDS approach of auditing countermeasures against intrusions. Much like virus technology, intrusion methods are actively being developed as long as new software is written, which can never be totally free of security relevant vulnerabilities. This is one way an IDS can be bypassed by an intruder, by exploiting an unidentified vulnerability for which intrusion attempts are not known and therefore not being monitored. But intruders also have a large disposal of methods available to commence well-known attacks in new forms that are not being detected by IDS. This is a very similar problem to the anti-virus detection problems with encryption and other machine language level tricks to perform identical virus tasks with new patterns, fooling pattern detecting scanners. When anti-virus software became popular, this game (or war, if you prefer) of evasion and detection started between virus programmers and anti-virus companies. Now that IDS are increasingly gaining popularity, it seems that similar evasion techniques are being actively developed to bypass them as well. It is obvious that there are fundamental weaknesses in today's approaches to intrusion detection. See [36] for some brief explanations on existing IDS evasion tactics. Something else to consider is, that people who configure, run and periodically maintain recent IDS are probably sufficiently enough aware of security to be sure to use updated and secure software (well, at least they should!) and will not be affected by most of the known vulnerability exploit attempts an IDS registers and reports. If being on the Internet, it is unavoidable to be scanned for vulnerabilities now or then, and therefore, false positives will accumulate, which alarm an administrator but pose no real threat. The problem here is, that if someone repeatedly hits your front door without the possibility of him getting inside, chances are that you will get weary of it, and, in case of a real break-in, be less alerted than you should. Sites that are most vulnerable to known security vulnerabilities often have insufficient time, knowledge, money or other resources available to be able to recognize and find these vulnerabilities. Unfortunately, such sites will probably not have IDS software installed, or even know about its existence. This shows that a coherent preventive solution may include usage of intrusion detection, but not as a single and ultimate auditing measure. Once suspicious audit trails are generated, by intrusion detection or other facilities, correct assessment of the event and appropriate actions will play the key role. To help in assessing such events, many independent facilities that each provide protection and audit information separately are of advantage. If you use IDS, I strongly recommend flexible, configurable software, because you can then perform a system auditing and disable configuration entries that cause false positive alarms [37]. In a perfect system, an administrator would have the ability to monitor all system events down to function calls and all user activity rigorously, but could chose to log only certain events at system and application level that can have a critical impact on security. Weak points of today's security technology include the lacking of continuous, permanent and fail-safe protection of a system at low level whose security and performance cannot be penetrated itself, and the enforcing of a restricted system environment that grants even the most privileged processes no complete control over the systems resources. These are obviously deficits which require new technological and systematic long term approaches and cannot be fully resolved using currently available standards and production software.

3.2.3   Backdoors and trojan horses

There will always be possible scenarios in which your system can be fully compromised, be it by a new, unidentified vulnerability, or by a vulnerability that has been overlooked or exploited before security measures and updates were applied. Therefore, awareness of existing methods of intrusion software - which can be designed to help an intruder keep full access to a system, including self-hiding, audit trail suppression, manipulation of any data that can assist in discovering compromises and assuring anonymity to the intruder - has to be created, before effective and (hopefully) reliable countermeasures against a compromise can be taken. By asking yourself what an intruder could possibly do after a full root compromise, one realizes that regarding the security impact, there is not much difference to physical access, at least if today's broadly used operating system software is used. Don't think that trying to discover known types of backdoors helps you to reliably recover from an incident (see 2.4), but it is necessary to actually find out that your system has in fact been compromised.
Scheduling scripts using cron(8) or at(1) which scan for access and change time stamps can sometimes help to find traces of unauthorized access [38]. A backdoor is any executable code that is used to grant an intruder access to a system without having to go through authentication, and possibly evades creation of audit trails. It can exist in form of executable programs, kernel code, or subtle configuration changes that help to bypass authentication. Popular ways of launching backdoors are running them on system start via altered SysV init scripts, preference files, or the inetd.conf file, which decides what programs to start on connection requests to a service port. Trojans are programs that serve a legit purpose, while performing unauthorized tasks such as letting an intruder gain access on special conditions which the intruder can generate. These kinds of trojans are mostly hidden in recompiled network daemons, and can sometimes be found by searching for phrases in the binary that seem to be passwords or encrypted strings (this will only work if a backdoor password is stored in a character string buffer, else the executable would need to be debugged, traced or reverse engineered). System access backdoors which are not created using trojaned executables or configuration normally run as own processes which offer some kind of remote access to an attacker (excluding privileges elevating backdoors on multi-user systems, which are mostly hidden in suid/sgid binaries). Therefore, a way of detecting a compromise can be analysis of the netstat(8) output, or using lsof(8) to determine which program utilizes certain ports and other resources. Traffic to destination ports that are not associated with known services running on the target machine, which can be found by using the above mentioned tools, or analyzing SNMP and router logs statistics can be a sign of intrusions. However, if a host is compromised, an intruder could have taken care to manipulate analyzing programs and audit trails so that his traffic is not visible from the host. It is also possible that intruders set up 'booby trap' programs, trojans of system utilities that are frequently used by administrators (ps, du, ls, who, etc.) which primarily hide output that would be compromising for the intruder, but can also be

manipulated to do unwanted things when being called with administrator privileges (alarm the intruder, change files, open a backdoor, etc.).
As a general preventive measure for detecting trojans, it is recommended to watch network traffic and system events from the beginning on, determining statistically averages of normal network usage. After such an average profile of network events is generated, one could perform penetrations in form of Denial Of Service and exploit attempts and watch for significant changes in the networks traffic flow. When real intrusions or intrusion attempts occur that are not specially being monitored for, a prepared administrator will have better chances of recognizing them by comparing statistical irregularities. This method might be gaining importance as stealthier methods to commence intrusions and to establish backdoor access become popular [39]. Using the present security level features of operating systems can also be recommended, to prevent interfering with specially protected files, devices or performing other privileged tasks as root that should not be possible to do without physical access. Secure levels can restrict the privileges of the root account so that it is not possible to do everything possible for the kernel with highest user privileges. However, mind that by rebooting to a different environment, this is still possible, because administrators having console access must be able to use these privileges (for example, to add or remove files and reconfigure the system). If you rely on security levels, it is mandatory to prevent your system from loading the operating system after being rebooted without user interaction at the console. You are strongly encouraged to set BIOS and other boot-time loader passwords; else, after a compromise, an intruder could remotely reboot the system into a insecure level, or with a kernel compiled by himself, instructing it to go back online after rebooting and granting the intruder remote, complete system access.

3.3   Conclusions about present security technology

As it seems, the security features of present software and networking structures are sufficient for achieving a secure environment, if some effort is put into the process of systematically securing, protecting and auditing systems. However, the present security features cannot guarantee that a system is safe from intrusions and other security relevant attacks with complete reliability. Not to mention the problems that many people have with security because they are lacking detailed technical knowledge, sufficient time or financial resources for establishing a sufficient network protection. There are obviously moderate deficits in the current information security architecture, which need to be resolved by finding and applying long-term solutions to the current software and network infrastructure to act against fundamental weaknesses which can currently be avoided but not completely eliminated.

4   Proposed future security architecture improvements

As both security technology and system intrusion methods are advancing, the situation is beginning to resemble a competitive race between different parties trying to improve white-hat technology and black-hat technology. Since the advancements in attack technology are happening unpredictably and many of the new intrusion methods are evolved without public disclosure, further security impacts and threats can not reliably be predicted. Therefore, the only approach for the future is to make coordinated efforts at improving the white-hat aspect of information technology, which can be done publicly with systematic, controlled approaches, in the best and most effective possible ways. The following proposals are aimed at programmers, free developers and companies, and also attempt to assist everyone who is unsatisfied with his present security architecture to point out possibilities of migrating to improved security standards. The main approach I will be taking is to identify basic weaknesses in the security model of the Internet and today's networks, and propose approaches to specifically work against these existent certain weaknesses.

4.1   Improving incident response capabilities

One of today's biggest organizational problems on the Internet is the uncontrolled flow of information. Because of the decentralized, non-authoritative nature of the Internet, information is being distributed over a variety of different channels, including security organizations, but also news groups, and media sites, which often do not provide reliable and complete information, causing unnecessary panic and paranoia on one hand, and insufficient awareness on the other. There exists a deficit in present incident response structures through which security relevant information is being gathered, evaluated and distributed.

4.1.1   A new approach to incident consulting

As technology increasingly tends to outstrip policy, user education and transparent information exchange are gaining importance. Incident Response Teams should no longer operate within restrictive guidelines. One of the most important tasks of incident response should be prevention. This should be realized by practical education and promotion of open security models. Security consulting should generate awareness that the 'security through obscurity' principle is not working against problems, but making things worse in the long term. Preventive measures should also include distribution of intrusion methods and tools, as well as long term weaknesses to the public. Generating awareness and educating people towards following the path of a hacker ensures that they themselves can realize appropriate security measures and recognize incidents and threats. It should also be mentioned that such a strategy could drastically reduce the expensiveness of information security in the future. [40] Incident response should aim to offer as many as possible different approaches and options to users regarding the solution to a problem. When offered many unique solutions, users can combine the different approaches and build scalable solutions. By being able to choose and weigh aspects of different options, they will also be motivated to get deeper into the details of the technology they use and might find new security solutions they can apply themselves. Another important service which incident response and emergency consulting should offer is informal and anonymous consulting. A big present problem is that especially companies are afraid of image and popularity loss when they have experienced compromises and should be releasing public information about it. If the task of showing such organizations that admitting to having security problems is the first step to improving their security is too hard, they should at least be assured that they can get anonymous consultation and emergency services, to help them in performing some 'first aid' security measures and to evaluate and distribute possibly valuable information about such incidents, which would have otherwise not been gained.

4.1.2   Incident response and law enforcement

Originally, incident response capabilities have been established by military or government agencies and big companies. One of their primary tasks was to collect notifications of intrusions, investigate (i.e. track down the responsible individual(s)) and, in most cases, to hand their information over to law enforcement. In my personal opinion, law enforcement should be reviewed critically when it comes to computer crime prevention. The reason is that the effects of law enforcement are, in this case, very limited. Intruders can be tracked, which however requires reasonable effort most of the time, not to mention the poor efficiency of computer crime trials, but the problem is that the possibility of incident occurrence is not related to single intruders, but to the level of security present on your network. If you manage to track down a particular individual compromising your security, but do not greatly improve your security after a security incident, chances are good that intrusions from other people keep occurring. Prevention of computer crime in general cannot be established by introducing harder penalties or better methods of law enforcement either, as deterring measures to prevent committing of crime can be considered as inefficient in this case [41], and a prevention system that relies on extensive reporting and countermeasures against any insignificant intrusion related activity could even lead to Internet security getting worse [42].

4.1.3   Establishing an incident response infrastructure

As a measure against developing intrusion technology, information exchange between institutions and organizations, companies and countries play a key role in early identification of new software, methods, and strategies adopted by intruders, which is essential for the security industry to keep up with them. Insights about methods that have individually proven to be successful against intrusion or attack methods need to be spread to improve global security. Incident Response Teams have to consider offering solutions that take common organizational problems into account like low budgets for security and fear of image loss. By designing solutions and emergency measures that are applicable despite of such problems of companies and organizations, incident response will assure helping a larger community, and incident response and consulting services will also gain popularity. In the same way in which security organizations and private Incident Response Teams should be cooperating with each other, an incident response structure should be established in form of a global security consortium, that coordinates information exchange between national, local, and private Incident Response Teams. If members from as many as possible countries would offer emergency consulting and incident response, while featuring 24 hour hotlines with real-time support, anonymous incident reporting, and incident reporting over the Internet using secure services, there would be an ideal flow of incident information, statistic information and latest security measures. Additionally, all options, including law enforcement, should be optional for help seeking attack victims, to enhance flexibility of the offered services, and different urgency levels and guidelines should be established, to assure that individual emergency incident response is available in wide spread or specifically imminent cases.

4.2   Operating systems

A coherent security architecture must be based on security established on different recursive layers of information processing. Strong security capabilities of the operating system are mandatory so that further security implementations in facilities such as network transport, user access handling and application stability can have reliable effects. The following section deals with some of the basic features that should be implemented at kernel level to enable high-level information handling facilities to provide a maximum of stability and protection to information systems.

4.2.1   Privilege separation and kernel-based security

Establishing security at system kernel level means to achieve optimal control, stability, and predictability of low level system events. For any truly secure operating system, it is therefore mandatory to use different security levels in which it can operate. At least two different modes of operation should be established, a maintenance mode, in which all systems resources can be freely accessed while being off-line, and a regular mode, in which the kernel will protect critical and fundamental system facilities and prevent any user or super-user intervention against these to assure basic system stability and security. [43]

The next security measure to apply to kernel design are better user-level privilege restrictions, to narrow down possible misuse of functions which are not supposed to be called in certain process- or privilege specific context. Privileges including the triggering of system events and access to resources and data need to be separated and managed individually by the administrator. If an access matrix could be created and managed, which controls access over all specific privileges, compartmented sets consisting of only the privileges necessary in each case could be delegated to specific processes and entities (different user levels / accounts). One set of permissions could, for example, be represented by the network family of functions, using access control to manage user level based privileges of opening different types of sockets, binding to privileged ports, or establishing active and passive connections. Additionally to determining privileges dependent from the file system flags of a binary and the authorization of the entity under which a process is run, dependence of other conditions should also be relevant to determine which privileges are delegated to a running process; for example, if the factual user ID does match the effective user ID, or if a process is running in a restricted (chroot()'ed, for example) environment. [44]

Further methods of hardening the operating systems core operations include methodological and structured kernel design, aiming at redundant security and verification layers, abstraction of different compartments of kernel tasks (I/O operations, cryptographic/mathematical operations, memory and resource access, network related functions), a maximum of facilities that can work and fail independently from system stability and security, and a kernel designed to use only completely defined, audited and documented operating methods to ensure reliable kernel behavior under all circumstances.

4.2.2   Kernel-based authentication

One of the big security weaknesses of systems exposed to the Internet are remote vulnerabilities of network daemons which can be exploited without even having finished the authentication stage of a service. Since the authentication methods of most service protocols are defined in detail via RFC and other established Internet standards, it would be possible to perform at least the authentication part of many sessions with a unified interface, just like incoming packets are all handled and processed equally by a systems protocol stack. I am only suggesting this as an optional solution to eliminating some of the widespread weaknesses in server software, and if authentication is applied at kernel level, it must not only be designed with security, but also availability, stability and performance in mind. In my proposed approach, authentication would be implemented in the protocol stack, and could be optionally enabled for certain services. The protocol stack would, after receiving a session request, act as a proxy and establish the session at kernel level after accurately identifying the client is making a valid request (for tcp services, by completing the 3-way protocol handshake), and before passing session control to the application authenticate the session using the authentication standard of the services protocol which is assigned to the destination port and then invoke the actual server application. From there, it could either, as a temporary solution be checked that the authentication fields contain sane values and the session including the initial authentication data is then passed to a traditional application, or as a better future method, the kernel would be passing an authentication token to a future server application which would start taking control of the session after the authentication stage. This service should be an option that can be activated as an alternative to traditional session initiation. If applied at kernel level, it could also take a unified approach at secure authentication and session key exchange via kerberos or other cryptographic challenge protocols [45]. The described method could, of course, also be applied to a system by implementing it into a multi-service network daemon similar to inetd(8).

4.2.3   Privilege and permission separation

4.2.3.1   Sand boxes versus protective cages

To effectively separate the privileges of a users' processes, a system needs to employ what I could be called access oriented design - kernel based access controls have to be present in a multi-user system architecture. This can be realized either with access oriented processes or access oriented user environments, which will be explained in detail below. The purpose of this design is not only to enforce access restriction but additionally the implementation of trusted paths, through which trusted information and executable content can be accessed and executed while being protected against manipulation of information, malicious code, and unwanted execution of generally unclassified or untrusted code. This concept could be called 'mandatory restricted code execution' and is especially necessary when using closed-source systems and applications where the user can not clearly determine the actions taken by a program, and to protect users against being tricked or forced into executing trojan and malicious code, that has either

been acquired or introduced by an intruder who manipulated the system.
In the "sand box" model, user processes are access oriented receiving only a
restricted set of resources and privileges, that forms a virtual environment
in which they operate. This prevents the processes from executing external
resources and any untrusted code that has not been approved as being a part
of the "sand box". An example for this is the Java Virtual Machine (tm) and
various script languages for web content which are executed at the client
side. However, these kind of restricted processes and especially shells are
hard to securely implement and to manage, they are overly confining and
they are based on a security design which can be overcome, if any aspect of
an allowed program, privilege or resource should accidentally allow to
execute arbitrary programs or code, breaking the restricted environment.
An alternative model is an access oriented user environment which delegates
privileges to each process based on access control guidelines and
restrictions related to user identification and the trusted state of binaries
and files. I refer to this model as the "protective cage", in which the
associated processes reside inside a protected environment with the full
set of functions and resources at their disposal (although access to
them is of course still being controlled at kernel level). To enforce
mandatory restricted code execution in this model, the system should maintain
a list of trusted system binaries and their cryptographic checksums. These
checksums could be kept in a special area of the file system or configuration
database file, and must never be able to be modified or created in the normal
system security level. To make changes to this database, physical interaction
should be necessary (e.g. rebooting the machine into maintenance mode and
operating at the physical console) for the super-user account to commit any
changes. In the normal system mode where critical resources are being
protected, the kernel must recognize such files and perform cryptographic
file integrity verification on them. If the cryptographic verification fails,
the files should be flagged as untrusted and therefore non-executable, and an
alert should be automatically issued so the original files can be restored by
the administrator. This protection is especially recommended to be applied to
setuid/setgid programs, shared libraries, kernel modules, system maintenance
tools, and servers that run with elevated privileges. It should also be used
to generate a restricted environment for users with elevated privileges, who
can then chose to activate the restricted environment (the "protective cage")
at any time, in order to be sure to only access trusted binaries which have
been initially approved. A feature which could greatly support this scheme
would be file system implementations which support new flags and file system
attributes which represent capabilities and privileges [46].

4.2.3.2 Differentiated access permissions

Separating access permissions to data and shared resources primarily serves
the purpose of achieving confidentiality for individual users. Cryptography
should be a standard feature of future file systems, to assure privacy, and
to prevent attacks aimed against the compromise of confidential data. This
approach should include time-based security, unique key creation for each
user, and transparent encryption and decryption features of the kernel
coupled with user specific data keys. That way, a separated access to
non-shared information resources on one system could be achieved, which
would help to mitigate the potential of race condition exploits and
espionage of security relevant or otherwise confidential information
left accidentally unprotected by users.

4.2.4   Auditing requirements

Kernel based auditing facilities are key factors for establishing fundamental
security and control on a system. One purpose of audit functions is to ensure
that critical parts of the system configuration, which can have impacts on
the machines security, meet certain security requirements in a way that
implements the desired security policy. Parts of the system configuration
compiled and implemented under individual human control (everything that is
variable, configurable and optional for the user) should be evaluated and
parsed in a restrictive way, that ensures fail-safe security. A systems
interface should not be counterintuitive, but its error tolerating and
tolerance features for arbitrary input must not exceed a maximum level beyond
which erroneous and insecure configuration can impact the systems security
measures, without refusing to accept such configurations or at least issue
clear and understandable warnings. A common problem for large sites is
to maintain secure configuration on a large amount of machines equally. My
suggesting is to design systems which accept and propagate site policies,
in form of distributed configuration management. A facility could implement
features to transfer configuration information and desired system condition
to other hosts on the network, cloning or reproducing a system state of one
host which has securely been configured and audited with scrutiny to other
machines on the network.
The second purpose of auditing is to generate audit trails, information about
system events, network- and user activity, which are needed to recapitulate
the flow of events and identify possible intrusions, configuration errors
and other critical irregularities. Though present logging facilities already
generate an overwhelming amount of information, they do not greatly
differentiate between regular, informational audit information and security
relevant (audit trails that can especially show the existence or absence of
intrusions and irregularities) as well as security critical (audit trails
which are created when system security or stability is being or has been
actively harmed) information. The monitoring of security significant events
should be focused on, and stored in a way that one can easy differ between
events showing unusual activity and information recording regular activity.
Ideally, a system should shall have the ability of recording all occurring
events down to single functions called at kernel level, and employ mechanisms
which let the user selectively and dynamically manage the types of audit
trails that the system should generate.
System events which should especially be audited and extensively documented
by auditing facilities include any processes initiated with elevated
privileges, and events that could intentionally or unintentionally generate
a point of access on a machine, such as binding to a port, handling data via
low layer sockets or system calls, and the receiving of network traffic.
These facilities must lay the foundation for the auditing requirements which
have to be further implemented at higher levels, such as system loggers,
process communication, and intrusion detection / auditing applications,
which are described in the following section.

4.3   Auditing software

4.3.1   Evolving intrusion detection

Since the first traffic loggers and port scan detectors had been designed, classical intrusion detection has been relying on monitoring network traffic and system events and identifying unusual actions and objects to determine intrusions. While this is a valuable concept, it does contain fundamental weaknesses (as described in 3.2.2) and has to be completed. Sophisticated attacks against a system which either employ evasion techniques [36] or try not to violate a given ruleset (for example, by gaining access from a trusted host and using compromised authentication data) can still very possibly be successful without even being noticed by classic detection methods. To substitute these weaknesses, future intrusion detection should be designed to detect intrusive events by employing heuristics. So, you should actively analyze all system actions and network traffic and intelligently determine what probably constitutes anomalous events. A sophisticated approach to intrusion detection heuristics would be to let an IDS analyze regular events on a network and supply it with hints about what could constitute an intrusion, in form of information about how different attack scenarios cause certain network and system events to occur, and in which contexts. An easier method would be to regard statistical anomalies as possible indications of an intrusion, outweighing occurrences of different events, depending on network throughput, connection states, errors reported by applications, etc. while differentiating between the severity of certain events, e.g. some events are regarded a less significant indicator for intrusions, so that it takes a huge amount of those events to trigger an actual match, and other events which are more security critical or more common and reliable indicators for intrusions are regarded as highly significant and trigger alerts after only few occurrences.
Future IDS should additionally be able to distinguish between different attack phases. [47]
IDS should react differently to these phases. While only internally recognizing initial information gathering, it should issue an alert when a system is being scanned intensively, and when an intrusion attempt is recognized that endangers system security, the intrusion system should, in addition to issuing an alert, actively facilitate corrective action to prevent impacts on security (depending on the kind of attack, filtering rules should be set, the intruders connection to the server should be terminated, or abusive access to a service should be revoked automatically). To determine at which point which action should be taken, threshold values, determining the maximum tolerable incident indicators, should be either configurable or determined by the IDS based on generic average values and the statistical analysis of traffic flow on the particular network on which it is operating. Another concept that is beneficial to intrusion detection operations is the ability to gain and evaluate the maximum amount of information about ongoing events as possible. Therefore, future IDS should work closer with audit trails produced at system and application level, and be generally designed as distributed applications, in form of remote network agents which gain and pre-process audit data and forward relevant information to a central, possibly dedicated host on which a IDS server is running and evaluating the different events by analyzing them in context.

4.3.2 Evolving proactive auditing technology

To verify the presence of robust and (mostly) impenetrable security measures, it is always advisable to perform active auditing in form of version and configuration reviews, and by testing servers and system protection. Since manual or systematic file auditing of the code base would be very costly and inefficient, the major part of these proactive auditing tasks should be carried out from the perspective of an intruder, namely, by scanning a system for possibilities to compromise its security. While current auditing scanners are already quite sophisticated and spot a large range of remote and local vulnerabilities and mis-configurations, a basic problem they suffer from is similar to the IDS problem; their scanning signatures have to be updated frequently, as new programs containing new vulnerabilities come out. Therefore, software distributors should be encouraged to publish auditing tools for their systems and applications, detecting especially insecure configurations, and to develop and maintain standardized vulnerability and mis-configuration pattern databases which can easily be implemented into auditing scanners.

Auditing should perform its task systematic and thorough, with the aim to support reliable configuration base design, which is especially important when scanning firewalls, intrusion detection system and trying to penetrate critical facilities such as system loggers. The penetration aspect of auditing should also always be implemented; nowadays, checking for immunity against latest Denial Of Service (e.g. fragmentation, land, syn floods) should be mandatory as well as either employing basic low level IDS evasion tactics to scan, or specifically penetrating and detecting IDS which suffer from such weaknesses. It is also recommended that an auditing tool uses a core part which gathers as much information about a system as possible (e.g. by recording all servers versions and remotely determinable configuration aspects) and then evaluates, determines and attempts to exploit certain present vulnerabilities with a separated evaluation part. The evaluation part of auditing software should be designed modular and extendable, as future necessity to detect new vulnerabilities is certain to come.

One of the biggest advantages for the black-hat system intruders is that they can carry out attacks and scans on a distributed basis. [48] Developing distributed aspects is an approach that scanning software should take as well, to scan internal networks completely. My suggestion for future scanners is to implement Internet worm like behavior into them. They could be constructed to take advantage of all existing vulnerabilities to spread through a network and identify its weaknesses, in a way simulating the behavior of real intruders. This means to take advantage of mis-configured proxy servers and protocol weaknesses to try to bypass firewall rules, exploit vulnerabilities in remote servers, then copy themselves onto the compromised systems, trying to get higher privileges by exploiting local vulnerabilities and then using the compromised systems resources to gain unauthorized access to trusted hosts and to carry on the scanning process from there. Naturally, the scanner has to be instructed to audit only a predefined domain or network range. I think the development of such an auditing tool would make an interesting open project, that could assist in improvement of coherent network auditing techniques, and also visualize the methodology of intruders and occurring security incidents on the Internet in a bigger scope.

4.4   Networking architecture

Originally, the Internet was designed for military and academic purposes, for researching, providing access to data over long distances, and as a communication infrastructure for a relatively small set of institutions and persons that knew and trusted each other. This scenario is the origin of the Internet's network structure as we know it today. Many of today's protocol standards for data transmission and packet switching have been designed in an environment in which essentially everyone was considered trustworthy. These standards can no longer satisfy today's ever-growing demands of industrial, civil and commercial applications. These traditional protocols and methods are still being deployed on the homogeneous, un-trusted Internet of today, while the rate of its members is drastically increasing, and its overall bandwidth is growing by nearly one hundred percent every year. Through the latest incidents and attack methods, it has become obvious that new standards have to be defined and implemented to suit the high performance and security demands of today and the future.

4.4.1   Routing security

4.4.1.1   Improving availability

With steadily growing bandwidth, the impact which intentional disturbances can have on network availability have become more serious than all other weaknesses and common malfunctions. Therefore, a central point of future routing technology has to be the prevention of intentional attacks by minimizing the opportunity for attackers to commence such attacks.
To protect against source address spoofing, all routers should perform mandatory sanity checks in form of forcibly blocking traffic coming from local network ports with foreign source addresses, and dropping packets for which no predetermined routes exist, when they experience large amounts of traffic with different source addresses that exceeds a threshold after which it is considered as a packet flooding attack which employs randomly forged IP source addresses, in order to assure better service for machines already known to have authentic IP addresses.
Approaches to preventing attack and optimizing traffic flow will often require expensive routing features, complicated algorithms for routing large amounts of traffic between different prefixes efficiently, and access control lists, while the use of these techniques can degrade the performance of routing significantly. To limit the necessity for increasingly sophisticated and expensive hardware, a solution should be designed that makes use of different multiprocessors to handle separate tasks.
For example, one processor (or one set of processors) takes care of maintaining, parsing and applying extensive routing policies to traffic, and the other processor is just instructed with the results (i.e. the defined route) and can concentrate on I/O operations for optimal traffic forwarding performance. An additional advantage that this concept could bear, is processors mutually substituting each other to prevent complete routing outages. For example, if the I/O forwarding processor would get overloaded, the other one would recognize that it is no longer responsive, and fall back to autonomous I/O forwarding mode, using static routing from a predefined set of restrictive backup routes, and if only the route-determining part would get overloaded, the I/O processor would also use this set to operate independently. The router could then also possibly reset the overloaded CPU and re-initialize it, without needing to reboot and interrupting any active traffic, while the remaining processor stays in emergency mode until the other one is back.
Another source of errors that have big impacts on network availability are misconfigurations in routing tables. Routers should encourage engineers to make extensive use of dynamic routes determined by the router, by presenting easy and feasible approaches for large and medium networks to migrate from

static routes. Static routing, mostly via plain RIP, is still too popular
and can cause big errors which are hard to track, if a large amount of route
configuration is done manually. Routers, in general, should be less error
tolerant when discovering that routes to unreachable hosts are set. [49]
A capability of the Internet Protocol are Type Of Service and Quality Of
Service facilities, which make it possible to set different priorities
for different kinds of data streams. These facilities should not only be
utilized to determine different types of sessions, but also to determine
different security and authentication levels of traffic. For example, traffic
from a host using a protocol which can reliably identify the host as the
authentic origin (such as IPSEC or IPv6), and traffic transported by
reliable connection-oriented protocols (after the session link has been
established) should be able to be routed with a higher TOS or QoS priority
on demand. This could improve availability of legit network traffic, while
the priority and therefore the impact of packet flooding attacks, which
mostly base on forged and connectionless traffic, could be reduced.

4.4.1.2 Improving access controls and authenticity

The authentication features which need to be improved are mostly of
internal nature (i.e. routing protocol related). Routers need to operate
in a stable and tamper proof manner, which includes that no data may be
manipulated from arbitrary sources. Therefore, cryptographic user and
session authorization should be mandatory for all future internal routing
protocols and administration interfaces.
Authenticity, in this case, is especially a problem when it comes to
reliable detection of the origin of traffic. IPv6 and other future
versions of protocols which implement security will improve the level
of authenticity. However, they cannot fully and immediately eliminate
these issues [50], therefore, measures of origin determination by
tracking back traffic (see also 3.1.3.2) have to be evolved additionally
to migrate to new protocol standards.
As it is known, actively tracing traffic back to its origin can be a
hard task. The issue is complicated due to co-operation problems with
other networks and due to the fact that the tracing process via routing
table information has to be done very quickly after the traffic is received
in order to be successful. My suggestion is to develop a fast, remotely
accessible traffic accounting facility which should be implemented in
the routers of Internet backbones and big networks which route global
traffic. Although read access to routing information is not generally
considered as confidential, it can reveal the internal routing structure
of networks, and may therefore be limited to authorized hosts. The routers
should each recognize the routers authorized for tracing directly connected
to them. A backtracking feature could work much like the RECORD_ROUTE
facility in ICMP, and could be implemented as follows.
An administrator logs into a router and requests origin information for
a packet which pretends to be coming from a certain address. The router then
determines from which external port, and therefore, from which directly
connected router the packet came. The router issues a request to that
router, which then determines its own port from which the packet entered.
That router then tries to query the next router, and the chain of queries is
followed until a router is reached which does not respond to backtracking
queries. If this is the case, the last backtracking router sends information
back to the router which originally requested a trace, submitting it the
address of the last determinable router. If such a feature would be developed

and actively implemented, an easy interface to gathering origin data, which would help to narrow down the real origin of any traffic, could be designed, which could represent an interesting alternative to the necessity of Internet-wide co-operation between backbone and service providers.

4.4.2   Protocol security

Improved Internet protocol standards, which offer enhanced integrity, confidentiality, and availability have already been due for some time. Internet transport and session layer protocols lay the foundation of network traffic, and if they have weaknesses, the chain of network security architecture consists of a weak link, at which it can be broken. Additionally to these issues, the currently available space for Internet addresses will not be sufficient anymore for a long time. In a period of as short as five years, all current IP addresses could be used up, and the industry will be forced to migrate. However, this weakness of IPv4 has had an impact on the Internet's infrastructure already [51].
However, many of the next generation protocols have actually been around for some time. Clearly defined and suitable standards for protocols like IPv6 already exist. They have been created more than two years ago, and offer transport-level encryption, reliable origin determination via authentication header (this does take care of spoofing attacks and reliable authentication of connectionless sessions), and different traffic priority levels. If two parties both employing these techniques communicate using these standards, high authentication and confidentiality demands can be satisfied. Therefore, it should be considered as an alternative to non-standardized VPN technology, which can often be quite expensive and hard to implement. Everyone is encouraged to make use of the new IP security standards, as migration is quite feasible [52]. IPv6 addresses are already being assigned by ARIN since 1999, and used on the Internet. Until the public breakthrough of the new version of IP, alternatives in form of IPSEC tunneling via IPv4 should strongly be considered. Besides implementing IPSEC capabilities at operating system or protocol stack level, there are other good approaches to implement IPSEC with a minimum of effort. Other security improved protocols worth mentioning include SDNS (Domain Name Service Protocol with secure authentication), ICMP next generation (which will be implemented along with IPv6), and RIP II (which can easily be employed in current networks and is strongly recommended for medium to large networks still using RIP I).
When it comes to introduction of security enhanced protocols, a fundamental problem the Internet society is facing is the lack of current Public Key standards and a Public Key Infrastructure, which are needed because a core aspect of the security features of security enhanced protocols is mostly cryptography using asymmetrical cryptography.

4.4.3   Public Key Infrastructure

One of the crucial reasons why there has not yet been a breakthrough in using IPv6 and other protocols based on public key cryptography on standard environments, are the difficulties in establishing a worldwide Public Key cryptography standard and infrastructure. Although PKI is an important matter and should therefore be standardized with scrutiny, a standard that is acceptable for everyone should be found as soon as possible, as the further development of the Internet depends on it. Apparently, there are more factors than only the technical aspect involved, for example national

cryptography laws and design of individual policies involving PKI.
The proposal in this paper, however, concentrates on the technical aspects
of implementing a PKI solution for Internet Key Exchange (IKE) which is
needed for transport-layer encryption and authentication, because this
could drastically improve general security standards on the Internet.
The basic requirements that an IKE solution should implement are a
transparent exchange of public host keys (so that it can be integrated
in applications and protocol stacks), providing authentic verification
of the key exchange servers, and a distributed design that makes a
decentralized key server structure possible. One of the currently
proposed protocols is ISAKMP, which makes use of cryptographic
challenges and signatures to authenticate requests, and can be used for
exchanging keys for arbitrary algorithms and protocols. While ISAKMP
could become a good choice for exchange of public keys for a variety
of different services with cryptographic authentication, it relies on the
existence of a hierarchical set of Certification Authorities [53]. Therefore,
alternatives should be considered for the key exchange of host keys.
The IPv6 Security Association, which is used to authenticate and encrypt
traffic at the transport layer, associates each host with a unique public
key identification number.
My suggestion is to use an improved version of the Domain Name Service
protocol to exchange public keys amongst the Internet, since the DNS protocol
is extremely suitable for associating a unique value with a certain Internet
address. Additionally, there is already a working DNS zone hierarchy
present on the Internet, which eliminates the inevitable necessity of a
global Certification Authority infrastructure. A new DNS protocol version,
which employs key- or challenge-based authentication would be sufficiently
secure to authenticate domain name servers as being authoritative for a
specific domain, and for the keys associated with the hosts on that domain.
This system would additionally improve protection against spoofing attacks
which involve attacks against the Domain Name System, and there are good
technical approaches present to implement it [54].
The Security Parameter Index could then contain information about the
authoritative DNS records. In this model, the registration of new
IP addresses could also contain public key generation and assignment
on authoritative Domain Name Servers by address registration centers with
local, national or worldwide authority for the assigning of IP addresses.

4.5   Improving software design

Nearly every information security problem of the past has been a result
of vulnerable, insecure or otherwise weak software. Conceptual approaches
to the design of standards and software have been done with merchantability,
ease of use, and ease of implementation in mind. While such concepts are
good, they should never lead to security and stability issues being
disregarded. Within this scenario, better approaches to developing, designing
and implementing code are essential. The following section will offer
approaches to systematically designing and assessing secure software, and
point out some of the most important security considerations that
should be made in the basic security design for software.

4.5.1   Technology standards

A major deficit of today's technological standards are vague specifications and lack of technical detail. When a new protocol architecture is being described, software developers should at least given hint about where possible caveats and vulnerabilities could be present. Often, developers have to analyze such weaknesses themselves when designing software that should suit new standards. Since standards generally take time to fully understand and to implement, people who implement them should at least be given support in the form of descriptions in the nature of a standard, along with their strengths and weaknesses. As a positive side effect, this requires designers of standards to analyze and rethink details of their technical proposals. Drafts for completely new concepts should also contain the descriptions of mechanisms that can systematically help to eliminate weaknesses and security hazards. It is suggested that they at least describe one valid, complete configuration of a functional software implementation under which no fundamental security vulnerabilities are present.

Developers and software vendors should always be given the opportunity to use identical interfaces and methods for their implementations. That way, a security and usage policy determined suitable for one product could affect security for other products and could be universally applicable, without having to regard technical differences on specific platforms or brands. Technical concepts which leave the definitions of exact structures and methods of a programming standard to the developers will result in products based on the same standards which are factually different in detail, and possibly in error susceptible code. Examples include the network file system, remote procedure calls and other applications using the early external data representation standard as well as early versions of Internet smtp agents. For organizations and communities which are actively developing production standards, it is strongly recommended to include details and practical examples, and to think over the architectural design of standards in general to make sure that the concept is foolproof.

Something else that the stability of software industry is also relying on is the fast development of and agreement upon practical standards. If responsible organizations completely fail to develop such a particular standard in a special case, leaders in the software and security industry should be encouraged to cooperate with each other and develop a self-approved de facto standard which complies to the appropriate criteria. [55]

4.5.2   Network application security

Network applications should be designed with special care about their security, because they are generally supposed to be used in a non-trusted environment in which anyone can access them, and therefore exploit present weaknesses in their architecture. The security demands of network application include stability, integrity (i.e. they must be fool- and tamper proof), performance and confidentiality. The latter should be achieved by routine encryption of sessions using SSL or similar techniques. Cryptographic authentication is also an important issue, which should be used to enhance verification and authenticity insurance of transmissions on both client and server side, to prevent insertion and manipulation of traffic, and to generate audit trails whose content cannot be affected by bogus connections, and uses the cryptographic origin verification to generate a reliable transcript of all security events and the actual parties involved.

For this purpose, a challenge protocol should be used, for example Kerberos, that never sends actual authentication data in plaintext across the wire.

To design stable and reliably working programs, the complexity of source

code and functions should be reduced and kept on a minimal basis.
It is also a generally bad idea to introduce default configurations which
with a program runs. Flexibility and options can help a user to
customize the behavior of a program and therefore improve security in
detail where it is needed. The introduction of more intelligent and user
friendly configuration management would be beneficial, but is not required.
Instead, developers should hire people for the purpose of writing more
comprehensible documentation. The documentation should not only describe
the usage and features of a program, but try to explain the technical
methods it uses to fulfill its tasks. Educating users to understand the
programs they use can be a great method of improving security that should never
be underestimated. Networking daemons should ideally work in a secure, custom
environment, i.e. under a separate account with the minimum of privileges
needed to fulfill its task, to prevent access and possible compromise of
large parts of a systems resources by remote users.
A final important thing that should be mandatory for the development of all
networking applications is systematic auditing of the program. Developers
should try to systematically uncover all implementation flaws, beginning
with main features and supposedly fragile aspects of the program and
proceeding to data structures and overall layout.

4.5.3   Software development security design methodology

Despite all security improvements of access control measures, conceptual
design, policies and standard, the most important issue to consider is
the authoring of secure code. This can quite be a challenge for software
producers, while the actual difficulty of design methods are not the major
problem, but the fact that many programmers are unaware of these methods. The
following section will try to help programmers to recognize the basic aspects
that need to be considered for writing program code which is sufficiently
secure for the implementation of future applications and systems. First,
most programmers need to realize that security has nothing to do with
functionality. Most software vendors do not have standard security systems
for code creation and review in place. They are relying on a method of
software development that focuses on immediate results. While this approach
does lead to fast development of feature-rich software, it fails horribly at
implementing stability and reliability into the software's operations.
Before explaining in detail how to apply secure coding methodology, I am
going to explain where to apply it. It is mandatory to employ secure,
fail-safe coding practice when designing network daemons, suid/sgid
applications and all other software that runs with elevated privileges
(most commonly root in today's environments). Programs with elevated
privileges sit on security boundaries. Most of the time they take input
from other programs that have lower access privileges than they do.
This means, a program running with elevated privileges can, at worst,
be forced into executing arbitrary instructions that have the elevated
privileges of that program. This is the reason why such programs have to
be designed with extreme scrutiny. Generally, program security should
always be considered when writing program code, as code can and is often
being reused for completely different tasks and purposes.
Some basic guidelines for program design include writing simple code.
Avoiding complexity and reducing the code size greatly decreases the
amount of bugs and potential bugs in the form of weaknesses in your code.
Another crucial point is open design. Nobody should rely on security
through obscurity, as every publicly available program, even if it is

closed source, can be completely reverse engineered. Your code should also be comprehensible for yourself and others, so that code reuse is feasible without having to completely re-analyze it. To realize this, code should be well-structured and commented. When it comes to user interaction, programs should be easy to configure and control in a secure manner. They should also offer options to generate extensive audit trails for verification and event recapitulation purposes.

The default configuration of a program should be made fail-safe, i.e. so that it denies any form of access and disables extended features by default. Additionally, programs with elevated privileges should employ separation of privileges. Necessary privileges should only be gained or activated at different times in different routines or processes, and generally, the principle of least privilege should be enforced.

To get more into technical details, common programming mechanisms and functions should be evaded, along with using shared system resources, which all can increase the volatility of the program. Your own, already audited and approved, secure code should be frequently improved and reused in new programs. Inheritance of large, bulky types and functions which call sub functions themselves, should be avoided. Instead, code should be re-implemented where it is beneficial to overall program security. Outside input (as in users, network traffic, system signals and events) should generally be mistrusted, and even considered to be able to take direct malicious actions against a program at the worst time and in the worst way imaginable. Internal protective and preventive measures against vulnerabilities to which a program might be exposed due to its nature, should be implemented, for example in the form of sanity checks, excessive load- and internal resource usage quotas. Special methods and constructions that should be avoided at all costs include all non-bounds-checking functions, complex and foreign data handling algorithms, such as getopts(), string parsing operations without bounds checking, gethostbyname() (note: due to weaknesses in the current DNS protocol, hostnames should be determined via dual-reverse lookup, meaning that a normal query and an additional inverse query should be performed for each lookup), handling of symlinks and other special files, checking files before overwriting and accessing them and using secure, non-predictable temporary file names to prevent race conditions, preventing direct memory access and core file creation in critical situations, using real randomness and unpredictable random seed for random number generators, making sure that buffers are always bound with a terminating binary zero, setting timeouts on network operations, and running in a restricted (for example, chroot()'ed) environment, where possible.

Additionally to all these security precautions that can be taken, code auditing and reviewing is absolutely necessary to ensure the stability and security of programs, just as both preventive and proactive auditing have to be used to adequately secure a computer system. Code auditing includes trying to overflow every static buffer, creating all conceivable race-conditions, looking for exploitable vulnerabilities from the perspective of an intruder who tries to use weaknesses in the code to gain elevated privileges. Secondly, the code has to be audited systematically. This means to review every access to any functions and to any objects in the code, making sure that operations do not fail in the presence of an intelligent and malicious adversary who is trying to forcibly generate faults.

As a last bit of advice, it should be regarded that spotting bugs in a piece of software which is currently in production usually requires having other people test the code than those who designed it, to review it from an independent perspective.

5 Final words

I hope that this paper has been able to give you some insights pertaining to methods that can be used to improve information security in the future.
I know that the work on this subject was certainly interesting for me and helped me to better understand some security issues in context. I hope that my attempt to put different aspects and problems of today's security issues on the Internet into coherent context has been successful, and that the proposed solutions are useful and comprehensible as well.
The Internet is a medium with a high potential for development, however, one of the side effects is the unlimited flow of information. It is therefore quite important to use ones common sense and judgement, without being influenced by unreliable sources of information. This also means that authorities and established organizations as well as common standards should not blindly be trusted. Instead, relying on one's common sense to assess proposed and established solutions regarding criteria of security, economy and feasibility is essential. Static guidelines such as described in the rainbow books, early Internet standards and international standards represent the foundation of many parts of today's current security architecture.
However, some of these guidelines are no longer applicable to the dynamic, evolving Internet of today and need to be replaced or renewed.
Additionally, experience has shown that hierarchic and centralized structures, while normally being useful, are often weak points on the Internet whose structure itself promotes decentralization.
One should be aware that misinformation can spread quickly on the Internet and cause severe effects. Making up concepts such as Information Warfare, are, in my opinion, counterproductive, as focusing on educative approaches is generally much more beneficial to the Internet community than counting on scare tactics. For example, increased break-in rates into banks lacking fundamental security would not be considered as warfare, either. What can be considered as Information Warfare is mostly unrelated to information security issues on the Internet and should not be used to generate hysteria with little factual background in reality.
Authorities, especially among different governments, political groups, and the media have been propagating the solution to security problems in a way that promotes security through obscurity.
But I am confident that the society will tend to walk on the right way in the future.
Even simple or small solutions can help to improve security in general, if security issues and measures are identified and treated properly.

6 Footnotes: technical background, definitions and explanations

[1] Information security has to be understood as a process aiming to improve protection of confidentiality of information, protection against unauthorized access and modification of data and the protection of the availability of resources and services.

[2] I am applying the term 'intrusion software' to any kind of software that has the single and sole purpose of assaulting or gaining access, information or privileges to resources unauthorizedly, including vulnerability exploits, although it should be noted that they generally do not themselves represent a security issue, but can multiply a threat potential that exists due to a present security vulnerability.

[3] Distributed attack tools are a kind of software that allow processing of tasks using distributed resources, in this case with a malicious or intrusive intent, such as Denial Of Service.
References:
http://packetstorm.securify.com/distributed
http://www.cert.org/incident_notes/IN-99-07.html
http://www.cert.org/advisories/CA-99-17-denial-of-service-tools.html

[4] Resources is a very general term. In the context of this paper, consider them as server processes giving access to different privileges, available computer memory and processor time, different network capabilities and devices, and different kinds of confidential data.

[5] Known methods of security compromises take advantages of a small set of known vulnerability categories, such as weak system kernel protection of privileges, undefined behavior on exceptional conditions, unchecked data structure bounds / buffer overflowing, unreliable input parsing, configuration problems, unreliable access validation, and file/resource temporary access insecurity known as race conditions or atomicity errors.

[6] Access control is a concept that must be able to isolate the full access to a systems privileges and capabilities and delegate it selectively to different users, resources and processes. Without access control starting at the system kernel, access to a system could not be effectively authorized and validated, and a separation of privileges that can be gained by remote, local, and physical access to a computer system could not be achieved.

[7] As shown by Bruce Schneier and many others, cryptography can be applied to improve and secure numerous computing processes. Without access controls on a lower level, like a system kernel effectively enforcing basic security, most cryptographic measures would be futile because they could be circumvented on a lower level; for example, encryption keys and system encryption functions could be compromised.
References:
http://www.counterpane.com
"Applied Cryptography: Protocols, Algorithms, and Source Code in C"

by Bruce Schneier (John Wiley & Sons, 2nd edition, October 1995)

[8] I define a point of access as any feature or service that has the purpose of giving a user access to a systems resources - that is, privileges, data or access to other facilities or machines. Practically, a point of access is a remote server program, or a local running / suid application giving access to higher privileges and data. Every point of access must be considered as a possible source for security vulnerabilities and entry point for intrusions, while the highest possible access that can be gained through an access point is the complete set of system privileges the access points' compromisable process thread has at its disposal.

[9] Denial Of Service is a category of attacks aimed against availability of any resources. Exploits of structural weaknesses that result in DoS include packet flooding with superior bandwidth, syn flooding and other bogus service requests, and exploiting specific vulnerabilities in server or operating system software to crash it; while no unauthorized access is gained via those attacks, they are much easier to commence and sometimes only avoidable with expensive and extreme protective measures.

[10] Probes can consist of any unusual traffic to your networks host, such as connections from the same remote host to all of your services ports, unusual errors like reset connections, and incoming packets that seem not to serve the purpose of actively communicating with a known service. A Network Intrusion Detection System can help in identifying such irregularities, while it is, however, not completely reliable and leaves the duty of interpreting threat potential and imminence to you.

[11] Network egress filtering is a measure to identify and minimize incoming traffic with spoofed IP addresses and is accomplished by configuring your border routers to refuse incoming traffic from unassigned and unreachable (not present in global routing tables) hosts, and traffic with IP addresses that should not be coming from a specific router port (for example, source IP addresses from your local network coming from an outbound port). Network ingress filtering, as described in RFC2267, basically means not to permit traffic from an inbound port with source IP addresses other than from your local network emanating to external networks. While these measures cannot protect from DoS attacks or intrusions, they can be used as an extra facility for logging and detecting DoS and intrusion attempts that make use of spoofed IP addresses.
References:
RFC 2267 - Network Ingress Filtering: Defeating Denial of Service
    Attacks which employ IP Source Address Spoofing

[12] A loghost should be a secure machine with a minimum of remote access points to which log data is forwarded in real-time. To forward syslogd(8) traffic to a loghost, syslogd.conf entries like this one are added:
```
*.*                @loghost.mydomain.com
```
If you use Cisco routers, forward IOS system logs there as well:
```
service timestamps log datetime localtime
logging loghosts.ip.address
```

[13] Reliable remote OS identification can be done by querying a machine with a set of TCP packets to which response is undefined in official protocol standards, and identifying the operating system by evaluating the individual replies to these packets. This can be done with many auditing tools, and was originally implemented in Queso and nmap. To avoid remote identification, one has to use special firewalls or change the kernel behavior (for example, by modifying tcp_input.c in the Linux kernel). References:
http://www.insecure.org/nmap/
http://www.apostols.org/projectz/queso/

[14] A network information center provides authoritative administrative information about networks that belong to the Internet. Like Domain Name Services, it employs a hierarchical structure of NICs, InterNIC and ARIN being the highest authoritative source for information about domains and networks and information about further network information centers that provide information about local networks, such as RIPE, APNIC, and country specific sources (like whois.nic.).
A WHOIS query can be made using the UNIX tool whois, or simply by connecting to a NIC's whois server with a telnet connection to port 43, and entering a domain name, word, or network address to inquire about.

[15] The definition of the last trusted state before a compromise is a delicate subject. The most reliable backup is the backup made before the system was connected to any network in the first place. Before making a backup, one should briefly analyze the system, and perform a checksum comparison to ensure the trusted state of the system.

[16] An easy way to do this with md5 checksums and PGP would be:
find / -type f -exec md5sum '{}' \; > tmp ; pgpe -r me tmp -o checkfile
To verify system integrity, you would decrypt the file and check the file changes with md5sum -c checkfile.out from a trusted environment.

[17] Possessing only a small history of security vulnerabilities is solely a significant indicator for open-source software that can be audited and examined over a long time by a big group of people. While non-open-source cannot generally be considered as less secure, cases where only few vulnerabilities in such a system have been found yet are less significant, because spotting the same vulnerabilities in different software is much easier and performed faster if its source code is publicly available.

[18] Many recent security hazards were a result of vulnerabilities in software packages, which got fixed relatively soon after their release, but to which many large networks and companies were vulnerable, because they immediately installed new versions of operating system and software distributions after they had been released. 'Good' examples include vulnerabilities of the IMAP/POP mail application suite, Qpopper, recent Solaris 2 vulnerabilities, vulnerabilities in RedHat and SlackWare Linux distributions, beta versions of ProFTP/wu-ftp servers, KDE/Gnome programs, countless experimental CGI

scripts and many other cases.

[19] The method of authenticating access with passwords is a weak and
theoretically outdated security mechanism, and represents a fundamental
weakness in today's overall security architecture. Besides buffer
overflowing and password sniffing, brute force password cracking is one
of the most efficient and popular intrusion methods, for which many
local password crackers like John the ripper and session brute forcing
programs are out. A recently upcoming trend is to use distributed
technology to defeat even strong passwords; while distributed password
crackers such as Saltine are already public, in my opinion it is very
possible that distributed session brute forcing tools have already
privately been developed and can defeat most password authentication.
References:
http://www.false.com/security/john
http://www.thegrid.net/gravitino

[20] Password aging, which can be enabled in many authentication systems,
forces the password to expire and a new one to be chosen after a
specified amount of time. This reduces the risk of passwords being
brute-forced by front-door login attempts, password file cracking
or traffic sniffing, all of which takes an intruder a reasonable amount
of time to be successful. It is of course also required to enforce
the use of strong passwords to maximize the duration of brute force
attacks, in which every possible password combination is tried or
passwords from a wordlist are used to guess a password. This can be
done by enlarging the systems password dictionary file with bigger
word lists (it contains all passwords that cannot be chosen), and
by enforcing stronger criteria (length, mixed case, special characters).
An approach in which all this can be easily configured are authentication
systems that employ PAM (Pluggable Authentication Modules).
References:
Open Software Foundation RFC 86.0 - Unified Login with Pluggable
Authentication Modules (PAM)

[21] A quick approach to find common coding flaws is to search for use of
functions belonging to the strcpy, strcat, sprintf, gets and scanf families
in the C source code, in order to find possible buffer overflow
vulnerabilities, as shown by Aleph One. A more detailed analysis means to
specifically analyze functions which parse user and file input, and doing
process traces (e.g. to analyze the possibility of race conditions).
References:
Aleph One, "Smashing The Stack For Fun And Profit", Phrack Magazine,
Volume 7, Issue 49, File 14 of 16, 1996, www.phrack.com

[22] Real-time event monitoring software often comes with the feature of
remote management access. Any remote access represents a theoretical
vulnerability potential and should be avoided, most of all if you need
a high-security solution involving real-time monitoring. Besides the
categoric problems, there have been actual weaknesses of remote management
facilities, for example in older versions of the Checkpoint Firewall-1
Authentication Agent, which could, if poorly configured, be used to add

remote authentication access from any host without authorization.
References:
"fw1-lpsnoop.pl" - exploit against FW-1 Auth. Agent by acd@weirdness.net

[23] While remote scanning and auditing tools, which search vulnerabilities in
a way an intruder would do (i.e. proactively), have been around for some
time, they have been gaining popularity since 1994, when it became popular
using such methods to improve system security, and they were started being
used by an increasing number of people to actually gain unauthorized access.
A pioneering paper is certainly "Improving the Security of Your Site by
Breaking Into it", which was developed in parallel to SATAN, one of the first
publicly used security scanners. This paper also already identified the
main problem of vulnerability scanning; that new vulnerabilities appear
frequently and scanners have to be updated to include detection of those
vulnerabilities. My private humble approach, NSAT, attempts not to scan for
known holes only, but for the presence and versions of remote services,
with the aim of producing detailed, vulnerability-independent scan and
exploit result logfiles that leave a maximum of possibility to evaluate
them for the user. (Ahem ok, a little, cough, private advertisement here ;)
There are many other good freeware programs out with databases that are
being frequently updated with new vulnerabilities, of course...).
References:
http://packetstorm.securify.com/docs/hack/security.html
http://packetstorm.securify.com/UNIX/audit/saint-1.4.1.tar.gz
http://packetstorm.securify.com/UNIX/scanners/nsat-1.11.tgz
http://packetstorm.securify.com/UNIX/audit/nessus/nessus-0.99.2.tar.gz

[24] A definitive guide to protecting confidential data locally is
"Anonymizing UNIX Systems" written by van Hauser of THC, which describes
how to reconfigure a Unix operating system to resemble a confidential
and anonymous source for multi-user information exchange and storage,
while in my opinion it also exposes that today's operating system
technology is lacking basic data confidentiality achievement standards.
References:
http://www.infowar.co.uk/thc/files/thc/anonymous-unix.html

[25] To penetrate a networks availability via DoS, almost any compromised
system is a big advantage for an intruder, who can use the systems
resources / bandwidth and the anonymity to hide his true origin in an
attack against you. Therefore, the problem of Internet security has
to be seen in a bigger context; the security infrastructure of all
systems has to be improved to effectively protect single systems.

[26] A popular application-/system-based DoS attack, the SYN flood, consists
of sending spoofed packets representing tcp connection attempts,
resulting in filled up tcp connection tables and unresponsive tcp
services due to many half-completed connections at the victim's site. The
cryptographic challenge protocol known as SYN cookies authenticates real
connection attempts, dropping spoofed packets from sources that
remain unauthenticated for a certain amount of time.

[27] There exists a technique called firewalking, named after the

auditing tool by Mike Schiffman, that can reliably predict which protocols will pass a point behind a filtering gateway, and which tcp/udp ports on firewalled systems are open, by sending tcp or udp packets with a IP TTL value that causes the packets to expire just before they reach their final destination, thus sending back an ICMP_TIME_EXCEEDED reply to the firewalking source host. Therefore it is recommended to prevent emanation of these ICMP messages to external networks.
References:
http://www.packetfactory.net/firewalk

[28] Simple Network Management Protocol is a universal protocol that can be used to record various information and statistics about network configuration and traffic. It can, for example, assist in detecting sources of high traffic coming from or to your network. However, by default, SNMP is using no password authentication, and UDP sessions, which can easily be spoofed. A MIB (Management Information Base) can contain sensitive information and remote access to routing interfaces, connection tables, plaintext passwords, administrative info, system configuration, and even remote command execution, all of which can be compromised. Using the most secure configuration available must therefore be mandatory, i.e. SNMPv2 with password protection, no default MIB names, no remotely writable MIBs, strong passwords, and filtering of traffic to SNMP facilities. There are also free auditing / brute forcing tools out which can be used to secure (or compromise) SNMP servers, like snmpwalk(1) (which has become a common unix system command on many systems), and the snmp scanning and wordlist brute forcing tool by ADM.
References:
ftp://adm.freelsd.net/pub/ADM/ADMsnmp.0.1.tar.gz

[29] TCP interception is a feature introduced by Cisco routers, but possibly present on products from other vendors which can be used to mitigate the impact of TCP SYN flooding attacks. A router that uses this feature will act as a proxy, responding to a remotely initiated tcp connection attempt in the first place, and only relaying it to the actual hosts when it has been established. By utilizing the bigger connection tables routers have at their disposal, and allowing minimal connection timeout values, the tcp interception feature can, if properly configured, help to withstand moderate SYN floods.
References:
http://www.cisco.com/univercd/cc/td/doc/product/software/ios113ed/113ed/113ed_cr/secur_c /scprt3/scdenial.htm

[30] For high availability it is advisable to block tcp/udp ports of services which should not or do not need to be available to the rest of the Internet, because they could be penetrated from external hosts, harming internal network availability, or specific services could be used to multiply an attackers bandwidth, e.g. if a connectionless service replies with a larger amount of data than is needed for the initial service request. An example DoS can be commenced using forged bind queries (but note that the external DNS, i.e. the nameserver authoritative for your domain must be available from the whole Internet!).

[31] Patterns that can indicate DoS attacks include unusually high amounts of packets of any protocol, but most of all ICMP (because DoS often generates ICMP error messages or echo replies). Further patterns include many tcp or udp packets with sequentially incrementing or decrementing destination ports, or destination ports that appear to be unused or random, and icmp/udp traffic coming from sites that don't block directed broadcast traffic, which is detectable by searching for incoming packets that seem to come from different hosts on the same subnet, or by comparing suspicious IP addresses with public known-broadcast databases from projects which periodically scan the complete Internet broadcast address range (see references below) or probing the sources' IP broadcast addresses for multiple replies from different hosts (seen as DUP's if using ping(8)).
References:
http://www.netscan.org
http://users.quadrunner.com/chuegen/smurf.cgi
http://www.powertech.no/smurf

[32] The figure below shows how a DoS attack commenced by a distributed attack tool (floodnet) would need to be traced back. This particular trace would require coordination with at least two other networks, on which the distributed software is installed, and all backbone providers responsible for routers between the attack victim and one of the flood daemons, and the backbone providers responsible for the routers between the flood daemon and the master server or controlling client, if the distributed tool would employ forged IP addresses in its client/server communication process.
(Note: I know that my ascii drawing style sucks, my apologies :)

```
[ Attack Victim ] <---- Incoming packets with spoofed IP source address
      |                 ^^^
      |                   ^^^ sending out DoS packets
      \-- hop-by-hop trace --> [ Flood daemon ]
                  |           ^^^  client/server traffic,
                  |           ^^^  possibly also spoofed
                  \-- trace -> [ Master control server ]
                              |
                              | By watching outgoing
   Fig. 1: Tracing Flood Network attacks from      \ traffic, or examining
       the perspective of a victim      files on the server, the other
       of a distributed DoS attack      flood daemons can now be found
```


[33] Recently, there have been reported incidents that NIC's were tricked via mail spoofing to change DNS authority records. Once this was done, attackers used their own, now authoritative DNS records to point domain names to different IP addresses, hijacking site traffic. A popular method of social engineering is also to create and post PGP keys or certificates carrying the same or a similar name as an authoritative institution, then using them for spreading trojans or whatever from 'trusted' sources. As it shows, services using hierarchical structured authorities inside the decentralized Internet are quite susceptible to such attacks.

[34] Another structural problem is that resources of hosts lacking security can be used by attackers to penetrate other, secure hosts and networks that

have nothing to do with the insecure ones. Multiplying attack potential through insecure systems for DoS purposes has its own history, starting with forged connections between udp services (chargen, echo, etc.), smurf attacks, compromising systems to scan or flood other systems, and lately distributed DoS, and exploiting, for example, DNS service or the MacOS9 protocol stack to multiply bandwidth, using hosts completely unrelated to a victims site to penetrate it.

[35] Since being developed and discovered in 1983, computer viruses and worms have been propagating in executable files, boot sector code, ansi characters, system libraries, interpreted scripts, vulnerability bulk scanning and exploiting packages, news groups, web documents and scripts, document macros and interpreted html code. They've been using everything from basic machine code instructions to script and system API functions to operate, and there are several thousand different viruses, which all use slightly different techniques to operate. All completely new virus code being invented has its own, new and unique pattern. As shown by the theorem of Dr. Fred B. Cohen, due to the nature of viruses, virus detection can never be reliable, as the occurrence of false positives and false negatives can never be completely eliminated.
References:
"A Short Course on Computer Viruses",
Dr. Fred B. Cohen, ASP Press, 1990

[36] There are already numerous different approaches to bypassing today's NIDS software, and I am sure that their number will increase further as intrusion detection gains more popularity. You might say that making use of these techniques is hard and requires technical knowledge and skill, however it is no problem to code intrusion software that employs these techniques in a sophisticated manner and makes them available to everyone using an easy program interface. Evasion tactics include using requests which are rfc compliant, but seldom to never used to get the same intrusion or scanning results (i.e. requests that are supported by servers but not used by most clients). Also, using non-rfc compliant, but silently supported requests that differ from normal sessions, or exploiting server bugs which make them accept non-compliant behavior can be used to fool ID systems; basically anything that uses different commands or data encoding has a high chance of being a pattern that works to accomplish the original server communication but is not being scanned for by many IDS. As IDS need to be optimized to parse much traffic, overloading an IDS with bogus connections can also distract its attention from you; moreover, it can even act as a network wide Denial Of Service, if a NIDS is required to process all traffic before it is forwarded. Another method with many possibilities is to use transmission protocol capabilities and options that are normally not encountered in normal sessions. Capabilities unexpected by IDS are IP fragmentation, TCP segmentation, IP and other protocol extra options, and traffic that looks invalid to the IDS but will be processed by the protocol stack and applications without causing sessions to end, for example fake SYN/FIN packets, TTL values, sequence numbers, overlapping tcp segments, and sending tcp packets which contain each only partial requests.
References:
"A look at whisker's anti-IDS tactics", rfp, http://www.wiretrip.net/rfp/
horizon, "Defeating Sniffers and Intrusion Detection Systems",
Phrack Magazine, Volume 8, Issue 54 Dec 25th, 1998, article 10 of 12

[37] Assume you are establishing network intrusion detection to protect an ISPs NOC hosts, being on the same class C subnet as dialup hosts. Nowadays, BO and other windows backdoor scans, or netbios sweeps are occurring very frequently on most dialup host subnets. However, if you run something like OpenBSD with high security, and now get hundreds of alarms that you are being scanned for windows holes (false positives), it distracts your attention from real problems. Keep in mind that not everyone has the time to find out how serious a particular intrusion attempt has to be taken (there are already thousands that most IDS scan for). Additionally, IDS logs should be kept small because they are generally checked on a daily basis if not more frequently. Therefore, my advice is to perform a system audit and only activate IDS alarms for attacks against services or protocols that you really use and especially ones that could be security critical. That way, you know that something serious might be going on when you are actually getting IDS alerts.

[38] Scanning for timestamp changes can indicate many of the intrusions that involve accessing (reading or listing) and modifying your trusted system data. Scanning for access/modification time and permission changes is easily done with the find(1) command, or using script languages like Perl or Tcl, which feature many functions for file examining and scanning. This tactic is even popular among intruders, who use this to detect activity by legit users or other intruders active on the same host. While this narrows down the possibilities of undetected activity, timestamps can be changed arbitrarily or copied from other files timestamps by anyone having write access to the file via touch(1) command or using the utime(2) function.
References:
http://mixter.void.ru/suspend.c

[39] Remote access backdoors do not necessarily have to use established network connections or open ports. As any technology advances, so does intrusion software. Backdoors can be listening on raw sockets, waiting for packets that match magic values, or that only make sense if decrypted with a secret pass phrase. Some example backdoors are ICMP tunneling backdoors, which have been around for some time, kernel module backdoors that can grant remote interactive or non-interactive access when receiving magic values in IP packets, or backdoors that listen to traffic on data link or raw protocol level. Examples of a remote access backdoor and a sniffer written by me, both featuring remote access on decrypted magic values, traffic encryption, and random communication protocols are Q, an on-demand shell daemon and e4d, a distributed sniffer.
References:
http://mixter.void.ru/Q-0.9.tgz
http://mixter.void.ru/e4d.tgz

[40] Thinking like a hacker includes questioning concepts, especially technological ones, and examine them in detail rather than just acquiring and using them. Note the difference between individuals I use to refer as intruders or attackers, who are in fact penetrating system security and might be using their hacker ambitions which help them in accomplishing this, or just could be using intrusion methods and software which almost

everyone could use. Educating users, employees and administrators to think and solve problems this way would be greatly beneficial to security, as many security problems and incidents which nowadays have to be worked against using extensive coordinated time and money resources, could be prevented and resolved individually if people were taught how to acquire appropriate technical background knowledge themselves.

[41] Law enforcement, when dealing with computer crime, is especially inefficient because it can be hard or even impossible to track an intruder. Intruders can strike from any country in which they are possibly safe from foreign law enforcement, and sophisticated intruders can and will cover their identity by traversing through compromised machines or manipulating phone networks. Additionally, active intruders seem to be very little afraid of being caught and possible consequences they would be facing, even when not being able to efficiently cover their tracks, as shown in the statements in the article by YTCracker, who is actively attacking systems. References:
http://www.hackernews.com/bufferoverflow/99/yesitis.html

[42] A growing amount of mis- and overreactions to scanning and probes is a doomed strategy that actually leads to security through obscurity. If anyone performing extensive network connections to acquire information about a system has to watch out for consequences, network security will no longer be transparent. This is an advantage to intruders, who can utilize previously compromised machines to hide their origin, but a big disadvantage to individuals who care about the security of systems. For example, I routinely examine servers before I do electronic financial transactions over them, to ensure that my information is safe from manipulations or eavesdropping. There have also been interesting scanning projects, which helped to discover and fix vulnerabilities, such as broadcast scanning (see [13]) or the Internet Auditing Project using BASS. Such beneficial projects are increasingly harder to perform using legit resources without having to think about possible consequences. References:
http://www.securityfocus.com/data/tools/network/bass-1.0.7.tar.gz

[43] Facilities whose protection is critical include file system attributes such as immutable or append-only which are used to protect trusted system binaries and audit trails from manipulations, as well as access to network interface capabilities and other special devices and resources like hard drives, read/write access to kernel memory, functions and control facilities, which all could, if accessed at low level with user or root privileges, be used to harm system security or stability.

[44] A general technical approach to establishing separation of user level privileges could be realized by a kernel performing verification of current access permissions as part of the built-in system calls, or a system in which the kernel checks the called function with parameters and the mandatory privileges of the calling process each time a process hands execution control to the kernel via interrupt with the request of calling a system function that can be managed using access control.

[45] Cryptographic challenge protocols can greatly improve authorization and confidentiality aspects of sessions. A challenge function such as Kerberos would consist of a client request which transmits an encrypted magic value to an authentication service. The authentication service then responds with a message digest (generated by a cryptographic one-way hash function) which contains the unique session identifier (or one-time password) and the magic value. The client then adds a secret known by the server and generates another digest which is sent to the actual server to establish a session. If both the unique session identifier and the secret match, the client is authenticated. In similar ways, a session encryption can be securely obtained over untrusted network links without having to be transmitted in plaintext and a secure session can be established.

[46] The current standard unix permissions consist of user and group ownership identification, read, write and execution privileges separated for owners, group members and others, and suid/sgid flags which instruct the kernel to initially start a program with its owners effective user or group identification and the related permissions. File system attributes which can only set by the super user at a low secure level include file immutable and append only prevention.
The POSIX file system privileges, which are proposed standard for the ext3 file system, already implement permission bits that assign privileges to do special networking operations (binding to privileged ports, opening raw sockets, accessing special files, etc.) to the process which is executed from a properly flagged binary.

[47] Intruders commonly structure their activity into different phases, and it is also often unavoidable for them to do so. For example, attackers first have to gain information about their targets by using dns zone transfers, ping sweeps, or connections to their services, then examining the versions and configurations of running servers and as the next step launch exploit attempts. While the first steps an attacker performs are legit network traffic which constitute no intrusion, they should be recognized by heuristic intrusion detection to flag further traffic from the same hosts to be monitored with increased attention.

[48] Vulnerability scans and compromises have been performed by intruders with distributed methods for a long time, while the actual use of distributed attack and intrusion software seems to be gaining popularity only recently. Intruders operate within a circular scheme; they first scan a host, then compromise it. Next, they install intrusion tools to hide themselves and commence further scans from their victims. The intruders use compromised resources at their disposal to perform further scans, sniffing attacks, and remote compromises from there. The more machines an intruder compromises, the larger is the amount of resources he can use for distributing scanning and compromising tasks amongst different computers, enabling him to seize control of more resources and so on.

[49] Misconfigurations, which are in this case represented by static routes which propagate reachability of certain networks through one gateway, but are unable to actually deliver the traffic reliably, can act as the cause

of major network congestion. Additionally, attackers can take advantage
of static routes which are less error tolerant by attacking gateways which
are configured to be accountable for a big amount of traffic. Therefore,
routers in general should be less error tolerant when it comes to
misconfigured and unreliable static routes, as mentioned in RFC 2725,
which consists of valuable information to improve routing security. It
should also be considered to develop advanced, open interfaces between
routers, so that they can remotely exchange information and policies to
determine if a route is allowed or appreciated by a remote Autonomous
System instead of routing statically and blindly without being able to
reliably predict if the traffic will ever reach its destination.
References:
RFC 2725 - Routing Policy System Security

[50] Migration from old to new protocol standards with improved security,
such as IPv6, will be done in partial steps, and networks based on
protocol standards with improved security features will therefore
require to be downward compatible until the migration is completed,
in order to be accessible by the rest of the Internet. Until this
compatibility is given, the possibility is left for attackers to
use old protocol versions to operate in networks with improved
security protocols in a way that they can still hide their origin.

[51] The Internet Protocol version 4 only reserves 32 bit for address storage.
This has lead to network address space tending to become rare, and
the establishment of some well-constructed, but temporary solutions,
for example Network Address Translation and Classless Inter-Domain Routing
(CIDR). CIDR employs a tactic that disregards the traditional separation
into network classes, making it possible to assign addresses to networks
with arbitrary amounts of hosts. However, CIDR concepts have drastically
affected the complexity of routing methods, and have caused some
confusion where they were applied improperly. Despite their usefulness,
such concepts have also weakened formerly coherent Internet structures.
For example, Routing Information Protocol version I, which is still the
most commonly deployed routing protocol, has not been designed to be
compliant with CIDR. The introduction of this concept therefore
made it necessary for many routers to employ new methods, or just use
static routes, which can represent structural weaknesses [49].
References:
RFC 1519 - Classless Inter-Domain Routing (CIDR):
        An Address Assignment and Aggregation Strategy

[52] As described by the concerning RFC, and already implemented in
existing solutions, IPSEC capabilities can be established either in form
of "Bump-in-the-stack" implementations, which are inserted at network
driver level, and transparently convert locally used traditional IPv4
traffic and traffic with IPSEC features deployed on the network.
Another method is the use of the "Bump-in-the-wire" implementation,
which employs similar transparent traffic conversion techniques at the
network interface by using dedicated cryptographic processor hardware.
Using the latter, it is also possible to establish traffic conversion
at the network border, by using a security gateway to verify and convert
IPSEC traffic to plain IPv4 before passing it to internal hosts, and

transparently converting outgoing traffic to IPSEC, making it possible
for hosts on the local network to continue using traditional IPv4.
References:
RFC 2401 - Security Architecture for the Internet Protocol

[53] Certification Authorities are a concept meant to generate a
hierarchical set of institutions which issue and authenticate public
keys. Each CA's authority and trust is verified by a higher CA,
leading to a structure of a Root CA and different lower authority
layers of Trust Centers, which register and assign public keys. The
have been problems of cooperation and administration that are presently
complicating the introduction of this concept, and the trustworthiness
and security of Certification Authorities are further issues. It should
be considered to establish a PKI concept without the inevitable necessity
of a working CA hierarchy, as the secure implementation of centralized
structures generally stands in conflict with the decentralized nature
of the Internet and is therefore hard to realize.
References:
RFC 2407 - The Internet IP Security Domain of Interpretation for ISAKMP
RFC 2408 - Internet Security Association and Key Management Protocol
RFC 2409 - The Internet Key Exchange (IKE)

[54] Using cryptographic authorization, association of public keys with IP
addresses would be more secure than the association of hostnames with
addresses currently is. The present DNS protocol is susceptible to
spoofing and insertion attacks, which could however be eliminated in next
generation DNS, using cryptography and high level authority public keys
for name servers to reliably verify the origin of each other. The DNS
protocol could then easily be enhanced by new DNS record types to request
public key and key ID transmission, as it was proposed in RFC 2539.
References:
RFC 2535 - Domain Name System Security Extensions
RFC 2539 - Storage of Diffie-Hellman Keys in the
        Domain Name System (DNS)

[55] For example, the International Standards Organization (ISO) had
recently decided not to standardize cryptographic algorithms for security
software and networking applications. Such decisions can throw back
technological efforts which depend on a certain standard being
developed. In such situations, developers should consider not to
rely on certain standard organizations, but work together with other
leaders in the industry to develop and deploy their own, self-approved
standards. Additionally, all developers are generally welcome to issue
RFC (Requests For Comments), a method, from which the Internet community
is always going to benefit, and which should be used by everyone when new
standards are necessary or desirable, but have not yet been formulated.

www.ingramcontent.com/pod-product-compliance
Lightning Source LLC
LaVergne TN
LVHW042259060326
832902LV00009B/1135